THE
KENNEDY
ASSASSINATION

The Ultimate Quiz Book

THE
KENNEDY
ASSASSINATION

The Ultimate Quiz Book

WILLIAM E. SCOTT

ISBN: 979-8-218-02544-1 (paperback) / 979-8-218-02543-4 (hardback) Darby Press

Title page photograph by Cecil Stoughton / John F. Kennedy Presidential Library and Museum

In memory of

Paul Sherwen
(1956–2018)

Andrew "Drew" Hadwal
(1957–2020)

Sid Mark
(1933–2022)

and

For my friend
Tom Belzer

CONTENTS

We in this country, in this generation, are—by destiny rather than choice—the watchmen on the walls of world freedom. We ask, therefore, that we may be worthy of our power and responsibility, that we may exercise our strength with wisdom and restraint, and that we may achieve in our time and for all time the ancient vision of "peace on earth, good will toward men." That must always be our goal, and the righteousness of our cause must always underlie our strength. For as was written long ago: "except the Lord keep the city, the watchman waketh but in vain."

From President John F. Kennedy's undelivered speech
Dallas, Texas
November 22, 1963

Acknowledgments

Two days after the death of President John F. Kennedy, I watched with my grandfather as Lee Harvey Oswald was gunned down by Jack Ruby in the basement of Dallas Police headquarters. It was like a scene from the gritty TV crime drama *87th Precinct*. Thank you, Pop, for allowing me to share with you that moment in history.

For their tireless and dogged coverage of the assassination and its aftermath, I would like to recognize the following print and broadcast journalists. Collectively, they changed the news industry forever. Among them were Elie Abel, Robert Abernethy, Pierce Allman, Ike Altgens, Tom Alyea, Hugh Aynesworth, Eddie Barker, Robert Baskin, Jack Beers, Jack Bell, Steve Bell, Nelson Benton, Jules Bergman, Kenneth Bernstein, Bill Beutel, Kent Biffle, David Brinkley, Bo Byers, Vivian Castleberry, John Chancellor, Bob Clark, Ron Cochran, Charles Collingwood, Frank Cormier, Walter Cronkite, James Darnell, Sid Davis, Gary DeLaune, Nancy Dickerson, Robert Donovan, Bill Downs, Hugh Downs, Richard Dudman, Ronnie Dugger, James Ewell, Jim Featherston, Bob Fleming, Charles Von Fremd, Don Gardiner, Don Goddard, Robert Goralski, Clint Grant, Peter Hackes, George Herman, Lisa Howard, Lonnie Hudkins, Bob Huffaker, Chet Huntley, Allan Jackson, Bob Jackson, Peter Jennings, Jim Jensen, Marvin Kalb, Seth Kantor, Eamon Kennedy, Douglas Kiker, Tom Kirkland, Charles Kuralt, Bill Lawrence, Jim Lehrer, Peter Lisagor, Joe Long, Bill Lord, Leonard Lyons, Robert MacNeil, Terrance McGarry, Frank McGee, Preston McGraw, Gordon McLendon, Marianne Means, Edward P. Morgan, Roger Mudd, Merrill Mueller, Charles Murphy, Roy Neal, Edwin Newman, Roy Nichols, Ike Pappas, Sam Pate, Darwin Payne, Tom Pettit, Robert Pierpoint, Gabe Pressman, Mike Rabun, Dan Rather, Harry Reasoner, Frank Reynolds, Chuck Roberts, John Rolfson, Bill Ryan, Harrison Salisbury, Ray Scherer, Bob Schieffer, David Schoumacher, Keith Shelton, Bert Shipp, Hugh Sidey, Ed Silverman, Tom Simmons, Merriman

Smith, Neil Strawser, Jerald terHorst, Russ Thornton, Dallas Townsend, Robert Trout, Richard Valeriani, Bob Walker, Barbara Walters, Jay Watson, Bob Welch, Tom Whelan, Tom Wicker, and Mary Woodward. To those I have failed to mention, please accept my apologies.

In researching this book, I utilized the primary and secondary sources of libraries in the Philadelphia area. I am particularly grateful for the assistance provided at Villanova University's Falvey Memorial Library, West Chester University's Francis Harvey Green Library, The Free Library of Philadelphia, Marple Public Library, and Springfield Township Library.

I would also like to express my sincere appreciation to Archives Specialist James B. Hill and Archivist Maryrose Grossman, at the John F. Kennedy Presidential Library and Museum for their time and effort in answering my many questions.

Throughout my life, family and friends have blessed me with their support and encouragement. They include George Bell, MD, Jerry Bennett, Reverend Barry Boyle, SJ, Bill Brennan, Joseph "Brownie" Brown, H. James Burgwyn, PhD, Betty Carboy, Louis Casciato, MS, Jeffrey Celebre, PhD, Charlotte Clarkson, Earl Davenport, Sister Immaculata DiBlasi, SHCJ, William Dienna, John Fawcett, MD, Tom Fitzpatrick, Eileen Frampton, Jane Frampton, Charles Ghapthion, Steve Ghicondes, Chris Glielmi, Robert Gorski, John Groch, Beverly Hadwal, Thomas Heston, PhD, Karen Katrinak, Dennis Kent, Kevin Kitchenman, Chuck Longo, Paul Lynch, Kendall Mattern, Noah May, MD, Levi McCall, Dolores McPoyle, Albert Melfi Sr., Joseph Micucci, PhD, Reverend Joseph Michini, SJ, John Milewski, John and Catherine Moore, William D. and Ella Moore, Nancy Moule, Rick Orme, Andrew Pauls, Ben Peters, PhD, Mari Preis, Daniel Patrick Scott, Pa-C, William and Helen Scott, Reverend Frank Skechus, SJ, Maryanne Sola, Carl Staub, MD, Reverend Vince Taggart, SJ, Richard Webster, PhD, Alice Welsh, Kerry Wetzel, Curt Wrzeszczynski, Carmella Young, and Al Zimmerman.

To my former students at St. Joseph's Preparatory School and Upper Darby High School, thank you for being a continuing source of inspiration: Chris Allen, Bill Avington, Stewart Barbera, Tony Braithwaite, Steve Calabro, David Chermol, John Connors, Craig Dimitri, Jake Ennis, Dave Falcone, Jenna Ficchi, Sean Gabaree, Nick Groch, Joe Ingemi, Joe Kain, Katie Karsh, Lan Le, Mike Liberati, Diana Lim, Jenny Ly, Brian Mann, George Marsden, John Martino,

Jackie McBride, Dave Mingey, Phil Press, John Regan, Katie Schlegel, Marc Schuster, Jason Schwartz, Jeremy Simon, Robert Sola, Lyndsay Taylor, Matt Thomas, Cherie Walters, Greg Wheelan, Donald Woods, Tim Wright, Patrick Zaleski, and Eric Zalewski.

To my wife, Diane, this is my last book, I promise. Well, maybe. Thank you for always being there when I need you.

Finally, I would like to acknowledge my dear friend and colleague, Jerome "Jerry" Taylor, who passed away on September 1, 2021, at the golden age of eighty-six. A gifted educator for over half a century, his was a life worth living and a life worth celebrating. The following is the eulogy I delivered at Jerry's memorial service on the twentieth anniversary of 9/11:

Good morning and thank you for being here. It seems only appropriate that on this day of national commemoration, we also remember Jerome D. Taylor, a gentle soul and distinguished academic, who epitomized the Jesuit mantra: "A Man for Others."

An insightful person once wrote that "a truly amazing educator is hard to find, difficult to part with, and impossible to forget." That was Jerry Taylor.

I first met Jerry at St. Joseph's Prep in 1983. He was the chairman of the history department, and I was a newly minted teacher. During our initial meeting… it became abundantly clear that his *modus operandi* was to put everyone he met at ease. "Good morning, Billy," he said (no one had called me that in twenty years). "Please call me Jerry. Can I get you a cup of coffee or tea…?" Thus began a personal and professional relationship that would last for the next thirty-eight years.

As shy and self-effacing as Jerry was, when he entered the classroom, he transformed into a bona fide superstar. The first time that I observed his Advance Placement American History seminar, it was clear that he was conducting a clinic. Jerry was a master chef who had created a recipe for learning. His ingredients included a dash of humor, a slice of sarcasm, a pinch of cause and effect, and a healthy portion of understanding and compassion for his young charges. Jerry wasn't teaching history; he was preparing his students for adulthood…He was teaching life lessons.

These lessons did not end at the classroom door. They continued in Jerry's office where he made *all* of his student-visitors feel that they were the center of his universe. And guess what? They were. I was always amazed by the number of current and past Preppers who stopped by to see Mr. Taylor. Lawyers, physicians, firefighters, restaurateurs, financiers, Annapolis and West Point cadets and graduates, teachers, police officers, and even an elected official or two, found their way to "Uncle Jerry's" inner sanctum.

I remember on one occasion, while sitting in his office, there was a knock at the door. It was a young lady whom Jerry had come to know through his association with the Prep summer school program some years earlier. It was not unusual for her to stop by periodically to seek Mr. Taylor's counsel. On this day, Jerry was experiencing one of his all-to-frequent migraines, and I asked if I should send her away. Jerry would have none of it. "If she could take two forms of public transportation to come here, what's a little headache?" That was the measure of the man.

Jerry's genuine affection and concern for his students was only exceeded by his love for and devotion to his wife, Linda; their sons Peter and John; and the most recent additions to the family, Peter's amazing wife, Meghan, and their son, David. I would be remiss if I did not also mention his "adopted daughters," Cindy, Amy, and Becky. To all of you, please be secure in the knowledge and find comfort in knowing that he will be with you always.

For nearly four decades, Jerome "Jerry" Taylor was an integral part of my life. It was an association I will always cherish…To me, he was a mentor, a confidante, and a father figure, as he was to each and every one of you.

A student of military history and an avid film buff, I recently rewatched the World War II motion picture *Patton*. In one poignant scene, the general, portrayed by George C. Scott, attends the funeral of his adjutant who had been killed during the Battle of El Guettar. As Patton caresses the cheek of his fallen aide, he ruefully says: "Captain Richard M. Jensen was a fine man, a fine officer, and he had no vices…I shall miss him a lot."

Over the past few days, I have given much thought to those words. Mr. Taylor, I shall miss *you* a lot, but I find comfort in knowing that you will always be a part of me, just as you will always be a part of "The Prep." Rest easy, my friend.

William E. Scott
Springfield, PA
June 2022

INTRODUCTION

In 1960, my family moved to the borough of Yeadon, a tight-knit suburban community of stone, brick, and stucco homes located six miles east of Philadelphia, Pennsylvania. With a population of less than twelve thousand, Yeadon was a slice of Americana. There you found the requisite number of barber shops, gas stations, and drug stores, as well as swim clubs, houses of worship and a movie theater where the proprietress, Mrs. Rhea Friedman, in her motherly way, served cookies and coffee to adults and dispensed popsicles to children during Saturday matinees.

Like most small towns, it celebrated Flag Day and the Fourth of July with parades, speeches, cookouts, and fireworks. During the Christmas season, Santa Claus rode atop a hook-and-ladder truck dispensing candy canes and greetings from the North Pole.

In retrospect, what made Yeadon truly exceptional were the people. They embodied many of the qualities that are lacking in present-day society—namely, benignity, selflessness, and empathy. I may be overstating the obvious, but it was a simpler time, when optimism was considered a virtue, and all things seemed possible.

Today, when driving through the old neighborhood, I harken back to my most memorable childhood days. Sadly, though, the one that stands front and center was not a day of joy, but one of indescribable sorrow and unbearable pain; it was the day when America began to lose its moral compass and gained an unwelcomed vulnerability: November 22, 1963.

For a generation of Americans that came of age during the "Turbulent Sixties," the quintessential question has always been "Where were you when President Kennedy was assassinated?" Like the Pearl Harbor and September 11th attacks, the death of JFK is seared into our national consciousness.

On that Friday in late November 1963, I was a student in Mrs. Fulmer's third-grade class at Bell Avenue Elementary School. As per usual, the day began with the Pledge of Allegiance and a few mundane announcements. What followed was an extended period of boredom. If I could survive until 3:00 p.m., it would be the start of the weekend, and all would be right with the world, but that was an excruciating five subjects and seven hours away.

To the best of my recollection, the day progressed rather smoothly, much to my relief. Then, at around 2:30 p.m., our arithmetic lesson was suddenly interrupted by a knock at the door. Not waiting for someone to respond, the school nurse burst into the classroom and motioned Mrs. Fulmer into the hallway.

After what seemed like an eternity, our teacher returned ashen-faced, and it was obvious that she had been crying. When a student in the first row asked if anything was wrong, Mrs. Fulmer hesitated for a moment, then slowly turned to the class and attempted to speak, but there were no words, only the sound of silence. Finally, after composing herself, and with great courage, she announced what thousands of other teachers were struggling to tell *their* students. "Children, may I have your attention. I have some painful news to share with you. Something terrible has happened to President Kennedy. He was shot and killed while riding in a motorcade in Dallas, Texas." Then, choking back tears, she added, "Please keep John-John and Caroline in your thoughts and prayers."

Within minutes, the principal announced on the intercom that classes were over and that we should go straight home. It was always a treat to leave school early, but not on that day or ever again.

Nearly six decades later, I can still call to mind many of the details of that infamous autumn afternoon, but I do not recall how my fellow classmates and I reacted after hearing the news, or maybe, I just don't want to. I believe it was much too overwhelming for our young minds to comprehend.

In the wee small hours of November 23, 1963, NBC anchorman David Brinkley summarized the feelings of a nation grappling to comprehend when he said, "It has all been shocking…In about four hours we had gone from President Kennedy in Dallas alive, to back in Washington dead, and a new president in his place. There is no more news here tonight and really no more to say, except that what has happened today as been just too much, too ugly, and too fast."[1]

Most people old enough to remember that day will tell you that it was like no other, but it was more than that. It was seventy-two mind-numbing hours when Americans of all ages were transfixed by the surreal and poignant images on their black-and-white TVs: the first CBS news flash, the shocking on-screen execution of the presumptive assassin, the tearful but stoic young widow following her husband's horse drawn caisson, the courageous little boy saluting his fallen father, the muffled cadence of the funeral drums, and the solemnity and precision of the burial ceremony at Arlington National Cemetery. Grieving as one, we witnessed a historic drama play out unedited and in real time.

In the wake of JFK's assassination and the murder of Lee Harvey Oswald, President Lyndon Johnson assembled an august panel of civil servants, known as the Warren Commission, to investigate the events in Dallas and to establish the "truth." But their nine-month inquiry did little to allay speculation that Kennedy may have been the victim of a conspiracy.

During the next ten years, the country experienced the murders of Martin Luther King and Senator Robert Kennedy, urban riots, racial injustice, the Vietnam War, and Watergate, all of which served to further erode our confidence and trust in the government and its institutions.

As we approach the sixtieth anniversary of the assassination, a considerable number of Americans continue to believe that President Kennedy was the victim of an organized plot. Ironically, when asked to identify possible conspirators and their motives, most have either no idea or mimic what they have learned in the dark recesses of an internet chat room.

After years of researching the medical, ballistic, and photographic evidence, studying the eyewitness testimony, weighing the single gunman vs. multiple shooter scenarios, and separating the logical from the illogical, I have reached the conclusion that the only assassin in Dealey Plaza was Lee Harvey Oswald. The facts are undeniable: the shots that killed JFK and wounded Governor Connally were fired from the building where he worked, he owned the rifle used in the assassination, he was the only employee to exit the building following the shooting, his pistol was linked to the murder of Patrolman J. D. Tippit, and finally, when approached by police, he resisted arrest.

Of course, this does not necessarily mean that Oswald was a lone wolf. He could have been motivated or manipulated by foreign or domestic forces that sought to remove Kennedy from office. There is a cornucopia of potential suspects, including the Mafia, CIA, anti-Castro Cubans, Fidel Castro, Lyndon Johnson, and the Soviet Union, but no conclusive proof of their complicity in the crime.

Because the charges against Oswald were never tested in a court of law (Jack Ruby saw to that), countless generations will undoubtedly continue to debate and speculate about what happened on November 22, 1963. One thing is certain, whether he was a lone assassin, a coconspirator, or a patsy, as he claimed, Lee Harvey Oswald, will remain, in the words of G. Robert Blakey, Chief Counsel for the House Assassinations Committee, "a mystery, wrapped up in an enigma, hidden behind a riddle."[2]

Since that fateful Friday in Mrs. Fulmer's third-grade class, my interest in the JFK assassination has never waned, and although my opinions have shifted over the years, I still regard it as a seminal moment in the life of our nation, and for that reason, it should remain a topic of conversation and robust historical debate.

In 1999, following considerable prodding by my students and colleagues at St. Joseph's Preparatory School, I authored my first book on the subject, *November 22, 1963: A Reference Guide to the JFK Assassination*. With a foreword by well-known forensic pathologist Cyril H. Wecht, MD, JD, it contains biographical sketches of over six hundred eyewitnesses, medical experts, and law enforcement and government officials as well as a comprehensive bibliography of some 2,300 books, periodicals, scholarly papers, and US government documents relating to the Kennedy investigation.

Why then another book about the JFK assassination? Beginning with the release of Thomas Buchanan's *Who Killed Kennedy?* in 1964, most of the literature has either dealt with the disputable findings of the Warren Commission or the endless array of conspiracy theories that run the gamut from plausible to downright absurd. There are very few publications that examine the facts of the crime and its aftermath in an unbiased and accurate manner.

With *The Kennedy Assassination: The Ultimate Quiz Book*, I have chosen to focus not on what *may* have happened, but what *did* happen (although there is a chapter on conspiracy theories). Using an objective approach, I have carefully crafted one thousand thought-provoking questions (and answers, if required) to test the reader's knowledge and to complement the already sizeable and diverse collection of materials dealing with the events in Dallas and beyond.

While many of the questions will be easy to answer, others will prove more challenging. For example:

- Who was the retired postal worker that plotted to kill President-elect John F. Kennedy in 1960?
- To whom did Lee Harvey Oswald propose marriage prior to Marina Prusakova?
- Who was the legendary business tycoon that once owned the theater where Oswald was apprehended?
- What was JFK's patient number at Parkland Hospital?
- Which English-born actor attended President Kennedy's funeral?
- Who was the only African American to serve as an assistant counsel on the Warren Commission?
- Which decorated World War II veteran and welterweight boxing champion testified at Jack Ruby's trial?
- What happened to the solid bronze Handley Britannia casket that bore JFK's remains from Dallas to Bethesda Naval Hospital?
- Who was the star of *Executive Action* that died four months before the film's theatrical release?
- In *The Ruby-Oswald Affair* by Alan Adelson, Jack Ruby appears in a photograph with which legendary country music artist?

Based on extensive research and with great attention to detail, *The Kennedy Assassination: The Ultimate Quiz Book* provides straightforward information on the essential aspects of JFK's murder. Meticulously written by a nationally recognized educator, it is a must-read for anyone interested in learning more about the puzzling and controversial death of an American political icon.

CHAPTER ONE

US Presidential Assassinations and Attempted Assassinations

US Presidential Assassinations

President Abraham Lincoln

1. John Wilkes Booth, the assassin of President Abraham Lincoln, was born on May 10, 1838, to Mary Ann Holmes and Junius Brutus Booth in _____.
   A. Bel Air, Maryland
   B. Richmond, Virginia
   C. Lexington, Kentucky
   D. Raleigh, North Carolina

2. In his youth, Booth attended which well-known preparatory school?
   A. St. Timothy's Hall
   B. Winthrop College
   C. St. Andrew's Hall
   D. Calvary Christian Academy

3. Demonstrating an interest in politics, Booth joined this political party in 1854.
   A. Whig
   B. Greenback
   C. Progressive
   D. Know Nothing

4. When Booth turned seventeen, he followed in the footsteps of his famous father and brother and became a(n) _____.
   A. poet
   B. actor
   C. soldier
   D. musician

5. Two years before the start of the Civil War, Booth witnessed the public execution of which radical abolitionist?
   A. John Brown
   B. Samuel Sharpe
   C. Frederick Douglass
   D. William Lloyd Garrison

6. A proslavery sympathizer, Booth blamed Lincoln for the deterioration of Southern society. Fearful of Lincoln's reelection in 1864, he conspired to _____.
   A. murder northern state representatives and their families
   B. kidnap Lincoln in exchange for Confederate prisoners of war
   C. lead an uprising at the Union prison camp in Elmira, New York
   D. hold Lincoln's youngest son, Tad, hostage in exchange for $500,000 in gold

7. Which was *not* considered a reason Booth changed his mind and instead plotted to assassinate Lincoln?
   A. The reelection of Lincoln to a second term
   B. Lincoln's plan to grant citizenship to former slaves
   C. Robert E. Lee's surrender at Appomattox Court House
   D. Lincoln's decision to arrest and imprison President Jefferson Davis

8. Booth's plan also included the assassination of Vice President Andrew Johnson and Secretary of State William Seward, but those attempts were botched by which coconspirators?
   A. Samuel Arnold and John Surratt
   B. David Herold and Edman Spangler
   C. George Atzerodt and Lewis Powell
   D. Michael O'Laughlen and Charles Evans

9. On the night of April 14, 1865, the president and first lady attended a play at Ford's Theatre entitled _____.
   A. *Our American Cousin*
   B. *Adventures of a Sailor*
   C. *Our Female American Cousins*
   D. *When the Spaniards Were Here*

10. Which of the following couples joined the Lincolns that evening?
    A. Emily Stone and John Milton Hay
    B. Julia Miles and Captain Samuel Shaw
    C. Mary Harlan and Robert Todd Lincoln
    D. Clara Harris and Major Henry Rathbone

11. Name the famous Union general who was invited to attend the performance but respectfully declined.
    A. Ulysses S. Grant
    B. Philip H. Sheridan
    C. William T. Sherman
    D. George B. McClellan

12. When the play began, which Washington Metropolitan police officer was protecting the presidential box?
    A. Peter West
    B. John Parker
    C. William Crook
    D. Edward Mullen

13. During intermission, the negligent officer abandoned his post. Where did he go?
    A. Star Saloon
    B. Martin's Tavern
    C. Greenback Saloon
    D. Cawley's Irish Pub

14. When Act II began, it was White House servant Charles Forbes who was standing guard. How was Booth able to maneuver past the unwitting Forbes?
    A. He stabbed him with a knife.
    B. He claimed that he had been drinking and could not locate his seat.
    C. He identified himself as a senator who had been summoned to the theatre.
    D. He said that there was an emergency and that Lincoln was needed at the White House.

15. Positioned within inches of Lincoln, Booth fired one shot from his _____ into the back of the president's head.
    A. Colt Avenger
    B. Ruger Hawkeye
    C. Philadelphia Deringer
    D. Bond Arms Snake Slayer

16. As Booth vaulted to the stage below, which cast member reportedly heard the assassin shout, "Sic Semper Tyrannis!" (Thus Always to Tyrants!)?[3]
    A. John Dillon
    B. Oscar Apfel
    C. Harry Hawk
    D. Victor Moore

17. How did Booth injure his leg before exiting the theatre?
    A. Climbing a ladder
    B. Landing on the stage
    C. Tripping over scenery
    D. Falling into the orchestra pit

18. Who was the first physician to come to the aid of Lincoln?
    A. Evan S. Hughes
    B. Charles A. Leale
    C. Bedford T. Morris
    D. Jacob G. Harrison

19. Because the president's wound was mortal, it was decided that he should not be moved to the White House but across the street to this public lodging.
    A. Blair House
    B. Petersen House
    C. Jefferson House
    D. Chesapeake House

20. With the government in a state of chaos, which member of Lincoln's cabinet became the *de facto* president?
    A. Vice President Andrew Johnson
    B. Secretary of War Edwin Stanton
    C. Postmaster General Montgomery Blair
    D. Secretary of the Treasury Salmon Chase

21. Including the other conspirators, how much did the US War Department offer for the capture of Booth?
    A. $75,000
    B. $95,000
    C. $100,000
    D. $200,000

22. How long did Lincoln survive before he succumbed to his gunshot wound?
    A. Four hours
    B. Nine hours
    C. Seven hours
    D. Eleven hours

23. On April 21, after several days of public mourning, Lincoln's body was transported by rail to its final resting place in _____.
    A. Columbus, Ohio
    B. Lawrence, Kansas
    C. Springfield, Illinois
    D. Hodgenville, Kentucky

24. Lincoln was interred in which cemetery on May 4, 1865?
    A. Oak Ridge
    B. Marymount
    C. Forest Memorial
    D. Evergreen Gardens

25. As news of Lincoln's assassination began to spread, Booth and fellow conspirator David Herold crossed into Maryland and headed for Surratt's Tavern. Why?
    A. They were looking for directions.
    B. They were looking for food and shelter.
    C. They were retrieving guns and whiskey.
    D. They were rendezvousing with other accomplices.

26. In the early-morning hours of April 15, Booth appeared at the home of Dr. Samuel Mudd, who attended to the assassin's fractured leg. Which of the following circumstantial evidence linked Mudd to the conspiracy?
    A. He denied knowing Booth.
    B. He was a Southern sympathizer.
    C. He had been seen in the company of Booth on several occasions.
    D. All of the above

27. Fearing capture, Booth and Herold moved on to the home of this Confederate officer.
    A. John Hughes
    B. William Lucas
    C. Thomas Yocum
    D. Ezra Hutchinson

28. On April 25, elements of the Sixteenth New York Cavalry cornered the fugitives in a barn on _____ in Port Royal, Virginia.
   A. Klein's Farm
   B. Reilly's Farm
   C. Miller's Farm
   D. Garrett's Farm

29. Before troopers set fire to the structure, Herold surrendered. What happened to Booth?
   A. He was shot and killed.
   B. He suffered a massive heart attack.
   C. He was trampled to death by a horse.
   D. He died of smoke inhalation when the barn was set afire.

30. Which of the following did Booth allegedly say before he died?[4]
   A. "If only for tomorrow."
   B. "The Confederacy will rise again."
   C. "Forgive me for what I have done."
   D. "Tell my mother, I die for my country."

31. Despite speculation that Booth was still alive, his remains were positively identified by Dr. Frederick May, who had previously performed surgery on Booth's _____.
   A. neck
   B. left foot
   C. forehead
   D. right knee

32. Following their arrest and trial, _____ of the conspirators were sentenced to death by hanging.
   A. Two
   B. Four
   C. Three
   D. Seven

33. Who was the only female involved in the plot and the first woman to be executed by the US government?
   A. Mary Surratt
   B. Molly Surratt
   C. Miriam Surratt
   D. Mildred Surratt

34. Along with Dr. Samuel Mudd, who were the other conspirators pardoned by President Andrew Johnson in 1869?
   A. John Surratt and David Herold
   B. Samuel Arnold and Edman Spangler
   C. David Herold and Michael O'Laughlen
   D. Michael O'Laughlen and Samuel Arnold

35. Claiming to be the last surviving witness to the Lincoln assassination, he appeared on the TV game show *I've Got a Secret* in 1956.
   A. Robert T. Dalton
   B. Jacob N. Johnson
   C. Benjamin I. Bristol
   D. Samuel J. Seymour

President James A. Garfield

36. Charles Julius Guiteau, the assassin of President James A. Garfield, was born on September 8, 1841, in _____.
   A. Elgin, Nebraska
   B. Sioux City, Iowa
   C. Freeport, Illinois
   D. Hugo, Minnesota

37. Guiteau, the son of Jane and Luther Guiteau, was the fourth of _____
children.
A. six
B. eight
C. twelve
D. fourteen

38. Having suffered most of her life from mental illness, Jane Guiteau
died prematurely in 1848. Which family member assumed Guiteau's
guardianship?
A. Sister
B. Father
C. Stepmother
D. Grandfather

39. As a young man, Guiteau received a small inheritance from his grandfather
to attend (the) _____ but failed to pass the entrance exam.
A. University of Iowa
B. Ohio State University
C. University of Michigan
D. Northwestern University

40. In 1860, Guiteau joined this free-love cult in New York state.
A. Oneida Community
B. Jefferson Dominion
C. St. Lawrence Village
D. Franklin Association

41. Disillusioned with communal life, Guiteau subsequently moved to
Chicago, where he pursued a career in _____.
A. law
B. finance
C. medicine
D. education

42. In 1869, Guiteau married Annie Bunn. Which was her occupation when they met?

A. Teacher

B. Librarian

C. Prostitute

D. Seamstress

43. The couple divorced five years later. Why?

A. Guiteau was an alcoholic.

B. Guiteau committed adultery.

C. Guiteau was mentally abusive.

D. Guiteau was guilty of abandonment.

44. Homeless and penniless, Guiteau moved in with his sister Frances and her husband. In which state did they live?

A. Maine

B. Vermont

C. Wisconsin

D. Minnesota

45. After attempting to assault Frances with an ax, Guiteau fled to New York, where he became a(n) _____.

A. minister

B. salesman

C. evangelist

D. sketch artist

46. In 1879, Guiteau authored a book entitled *The Truth* in which he plagiarized the ideas of this religious leader.

A. Brigham Young

B. Dwight Moody

C. Benjamin Warfield

D. John Humphrey Noyes

47. Turning to politics, Guiteau supported Congressman James Garfield's 1880 presidential bid by delivering speeches and writing a pamphlet entitled _____.
    A. *Good vs. Evil*
    B. *North vs. South*
    C. *Garfield vs. Hancock*
    D. *Freedmen vs. Redeemers*

48. Following the election, Guiteau, who felt partially responsible for Garfield's victory, petitioned the administration for a diplomatic post in _____.
    A. Japan or Italy
    B. Austria or France
    C. England or Russia
    D. Germany or Spain

49. Distraught over failing to secure an appointment, Guiteau claimed that he was "pressured" to kill Garfield by _____.
    A. God
    B. Thor
    C. Zeus
    D. Lucifer

50. After settling on his course of action, Guiteau purchased which of the following revolvers?
    A. Enfield Mk II
    B. Colt Dragoon
    C. Webley Shark
    D. British Bulldog

51. Guiteau initially considered using (a) _____ to assassinate the president.
    A. poison
    B. hammer
    C. dynamite
    D. crossbow

52. On the morning of July 2, 1881, Garfield was scheduled to travel by train to New England for commencement services at (the) _____.
    A. Williams College
    B. Colgate University
    C. Dartmouth College
    D. University of Vermont

53. Entering the Baltimore and Potomac Railroad Station at 9:30 a.m., Garfield was shot twice from behind by Guiteau. Collapsing to the floor, he cried out, _____ [5]
    A. "Who did it?"
    B. "No, it can't be!"
    C. "My God, what is that?"
    D. "Would someone please help me!"

54. The first of two bullets nicked the president's right arm. The second lodged in his _____.
    A. pelvis
    B. larynx
    C. scrotum
    D. abdomen

55. Who was the Washington physician that provided Garfield with questionable medical care?
    A. Willard Bliss
    B. Charles Purvis
    C. Smith Townsend
    D. Rutherford Simpson

56. According to author and journalist Candice Millard, which "instruments" were initially used to probe the president's wounds?
    A. Spatulas
    B. Corkscrews
    C. Kitchen knives
    D. Unclean hands

57. In a bizarre attempt to locate the second bullet, doctors tried a new invention by Alexander Graham Bell called a(n) _____.
    A. Geiger counter
    B. Metal detector
    C. Electron microscope
    D. Carbon thermometer

58. Although Garfield's gunshot wounds were not considered life threatening by today's standards, he nevertheless succumbed on September 19, 1881. Which factor(s) contributed to his death?
    A. Massive infection
    B. Substantial loss of blood
    C. Inadequate medical care
    D. A and C

59. Name the Washington Metropolitan Police officer who apprehended Guiteau following the shooting.
    A. John Fowler
    B. Francis Doyle
    C. Patrick Kearney
    D. Quincy Bradford

60. In his haste to capture the assassin, what did the policeman forget to do?
    A. Handcuff Guiteau
    B. Call for assistance
    C. Read Guiteau his rights
    D. Confiscate Guiteau's pistol

61. Which were the first words spoken by Guiteau after his arrest?[6]
    A. "The Lord has seen fit to elevate me to greatness!"
    B. "Let it be recorded that I alone slayed the evil one!"
    C. "I am a Stalwart of the Stalwarts…Arthur is president now!'"
    D. "A jury will find me not guilty. I was guided by the Almighty to commit this act!"

62. In the days following the shooting, Guiteau announced that he would write and publish a memoir entitled _____.
    A. *Charles Guiteau: An American Assassin*
    B. *The Life and Theology of Charles Guiteau*
    C. *Guiteau: The Man, the Myth, and the Legend*
    D. *The Life and Times of President Garfield's Assassin*

63. Following Garfield's death, Guiteau was indicted for murder on October 14, 1881. The trial began on _____.
    A. November 10, 1881
    B. November 14, 1881
    C. November 17, 1881
    D. November 19, 1881

64. Which of Guiteau's defense attorneys was also his brother-in-law?
    A. George Scoville
    B. Merrill Webber
    C. Leigh Robinson
    D. Clarence Brewer

65. The government's legal team was comprised of five New York and Washington lawyers, including one that would receive the Nobel Peace Prize in 1913. Who was he?
    A. Elihu Root
    B. Hamilton Fish
    C. Theodore Roosevelt
    D. William Jennings Bryan

66. Guiteau's defense was based on two assertions. Which were they?
    A. Guiteau was a patsy, and he had already been convicted in the press.
    B. Guiteau was part of an international conspiracy, and he suffered from a split personality.
    C. Guiteau was legally insane, and he did not kill Garfield; improper medical care caused his death.
    D. Guiteau was denied his First Amendment rights, and he was suffering from a personality disorder.

67. On January 25, 1882, following a two-month trial, the accused was found guilty of murdering Garfield. Upon hearing the guilty verdict, Guiteau berated the jurors and shouted, _____[7]
    A. "May you all burn in the bowels of hell!"
    B. "Fire and brimstone will be your reward!"
    C. "You are all low, consummate jackasses!"
    D. "A grinding and horrific death will be your fate!"

68. Prior to his execution, Guiteau wrote a poem. What was the title?
    A. "I am Going to the Lordy"
    B. "Dear God, Please Open the Pearly Gates"
    C. "I've Packed My Bags and I'm Ready to Go"
    D. "They Are All Gone into the World of Light"

69. By which means was Guiteau put to death on June 30, 1882?
    A. Hanging
    B. Firing squad
    C. Electrocution
    D. Lethal injection

70. Guiteau's postmortem strongly suggested that he may have suffered from _____.
    A. cancer
    B. syphilis
    C. leukemia
    D. sarcoidosis

71. What eventually happened to Guiteau's remains?
    A. They were returned to his family for burial.
    B. They were donated to the Smithsonian Institute.
    C. They were stolen by grave robbers and never recovered.
    D. They were given to the National Museum of Health and Medicine.

72. All the following resulted in the wake of Garfield's assassination *except* _____.
    A. civil service reform was enacted
    B. the nation grieved as one for its fallen leader
    C. American physicians acknowledged the need to use antiseptics
    D. federally elected officials were guaranteed full-time protection

President William McKinley

73. The assassin of President William McKinley, Leon Frank Czolgosz, was born on May 5, 1873, in _____.
    A. Salem, Oregon
    B. Wichita, Kansas
    C. Detroit, Michigan
    D. Altoona, Pennsylvania

74. Czolgosz, the son of Paul Czolgosz and Mary Nohawk, was the fourth of _____ children.
    A. ten
    B. eleven
    C. twelve
    D. fourteen

75. As a young man, Czolgosz became interested in _____.
    A. Fascism
    B. Socialism
    C. Anarchism
    D. Corporatism

76. Of the following, which was Czolgosz's motivation for assassinating President McKinley?
    A. He was convinced that the president was a Communist.
    B. He blamed the president for the nation's economic woes.
    C. He wanted to provoke a war between the US and Great Britain.
    D. He blamed the president for starting the Spanish-American War.

77. Where and when did Czolgosz plan to shoot the president?
    A. Midwestern Exposition in Cleveland, Ohio / July 4, 1901
    B. Pan-American Exposition in Buffalo, New York / September 6, 1901
    C. Eastern Industrial Exposition in Elkton, Maryland / October 18, 1901
    D. World Trade Exposition in Pittsburgh, Pennsylvania / August 24, 1901

78. His pistol of choice was the same used in the assassination of King
    Umberto I of Italy in 1900. Name the weapon.
    A. .38 Springfield
    B. .44 Wentworth
    C. .32 Iver Johnson
    D. .45 Colt Paterson

79. In which of the exposition's buildings did the assassination take place.
    A. Palace of Peace
    B. Shrine of Justice
    C. Hall of Freedom
    D. Temple of Music

80. Where did Czolgosz conceal his weapon before shooting McKinley?
    A. Umbrella
    B. Violin case
    C. Handkerchief
    D. Floral bouquet

81. As the assassin was subdued, what did the twice-wounded McKinley say?[8]
    A. "Let no one hurt him!"
    B. "Don't let him get away!"
    C. "I thought he was an admirer!"
    D. "Make certain that he pays for this!"

82. When did McKinley succumb to his wounds?
    A. Eight days later
    B. Twelve days later
    C. Fifteen days later
    D. Sixteen days later

83. On September 23, 1901, Czolgosz's murder trial began. How long did the proceedings last?
    A. Four hours
    B. Eight hours
    C. Twelve hours
    D. Fifteen hours

84. After less than thirty minutes of deliberation, the jury found Czolgosz guilty, and he was sentenced to death. By which means was he executed on October 29, 1901?
    A. Firing squad
    B. Electric chair
    C. Gas chamber
    D. Lethal injection

ATTEMPTED ASSASSINATIONS

85. The first attempt on the life of a sitting president occurred on January 30, 1835. Who was the intended victim?
    A. John Tyler
    B. Andrew Jackson
    C. John Quincy Adams
    D. William Henry Harrison

86. Name the former chief executive whose assassination was thwarted by a folded speech and an eyeglass case.
    A. William Taft
    B. Zachary Taylor
    C. Benjamin Harrison
    D. Theodore Roosevelt

87. Which of the following presidents was nearly killed when anarchists tried to blow-up his train?
    A. Calvin Coolidge
    B. Herbert Hoover
    C. Ulysses S. Grant
    D. Millard Fillmore

88. In 1933, a gun-toting assassin missed President-elect Franklin D. Roosevelt (FDR) and instead mortally wounded Chicago Mayor Anton Cermak. Who was he?
    A. Pietro Galleani
    B. Vincenzo Motta
    C. Giuseppe Zangara
    D. Enrico Gianncarlo

89. On December 8, 1941, the day after the Japanese attack on Pearl Harbor, FDR addressed a joint session of Congress. According to legend, the Secret Service, fearing an assassination attempt, transported Roosevelt to the US Capitol in a Cadillac sedan with bulletproof windows. Which mob kingpin once owned the vehicle?
    A. John "Lefty" O'Toole
    B. Al "Scarface" Capone
    C. George "Bugs" Moran
    D. Benjamin "Bugsy" Siegel

90. Name the two Puerto Rican nationalists who tried unsuccessfully to assassinate President Harry Truman in 1951.
    A. Luis Martinez and Samuel Munoz
    B. Juan Hernandez and Miguel Agosto
    C. Oscar Collazo and Griselio Torresola
    D. Antonio Morales and Rafael Sanchez

91. Buried in Arlington National Cemetery, he is the only member of the US Secret Service Uniformed Division to be killed while protecting a president.
    A. James M. Ryan
    B. Leslie W. Coffelt
    C. James A. Hollinger
    D. Thomas B. Shipman

92. In 1972, this controversial presidential candidate was shot multiple times by a mentally unstable felon named Arthur Bremer.
    A. Orval Faubus
    B. Lester Maddox
    C. George Wallace
    D. Buford Ellington

93. Of the following, who was Arthur Bremer's original target?
    A. Richard Nixon
    B. Edward Kennedy
    C. Hubert Humphrey
    D. George McGovern

94. Which was the code name for Samuel Joseph Byck's plan to crash a Delta DC-8 into the White House in 1974?
    A. "Operation Crossbow"
    B. "Operation Samuel Says"
    C. "Operation Pandora's Box"
    D. "Operation Executive Sanction"

95. Name the disciple of Charles Manson who made an assassination attempt on the life of the thirty-eighth president of the United States on September 5, 1975.
    A. Sandra Good
    B. Lynette Fromme
    C. Sara Jane Moore
    D. Leslie Van Houten

96. In 1979, this Ohio drifter claimed to be part of an organized plot to assassinate President Jimmy Carter.
   A. Lee Oswald Harvey
   B. Raymond Lee Harvey
   C. Harvey Lee Raymond
   D. Oswald Raymond Lee

97. All of the following were wounded in the shooting of President Ronald Reagan *except* _____.
   A. James Brady
   B. Timothy McCarthy
   C. Raymond Donovan
   D. Thomas Delahanty

98. How many documented attempts were there on the life of President Bill Clinton in 1994?
   A. One
   B. Two
   C. Five
   D. Seven

99. Three of these men were implicated in a plot to kill presidential nominee Barack Obama. Which one was *not* involved?
   A. Earl David Lee
   B. Shawn Robert Adolf
   C. Tharin Robert Gartrell
   D. Nathan Dwaine Johnson

100. In 2016, British tourist Michael Steven Sanford planned to use a policeman's gun to kill this presidential candidate.
   A. Ted Cruz
   B. Donald Trump
   C. Lindsay Graham
   D. Michael Bloomberg

Chapter One Answers

1. A. Bel Air, Maryland
2. A. St. Timothy's Hall
3. D. Know Nothing
4. B. actor
5. A. John Brown
6. B. kidnap Lincoln in exchange for Confederate prisoners of war
7. D. Lincoln's decision to arrest and imprison President Jefferson Davis
8. C. George Atzerodt and Lewis Powell
9. A. *Our American Cousin*
10. D. Clara Harris and Major Henry Rathbone
11. A. Ulysses S. Grant
12. B. John Parker
13. A. Star Saloon
14. C. He identified himself as a senator who had been summoned to the theatre.
15. C. Philadelphia Deringer
16. C. Harry Hawk
17. B. Landing on the stage
18. B. Charles A. Leale
19. B. Petersen House
20. B. Secretary of War Edwin Stanton
21. C. $100,000
22. B. Nine hours
23. C. Springfield, Illinois
24. A. Oak Ridge
25. C. They were retrieving guns and whiskey.
26. D. All of the above
27. A. John Hughes
28. D. Garrett's Farm
29. A. He was shot and killed.

30. D. "Tell my mother, I die for my country."
31. A. neck
32. B. Four
33. A. Mary Surratt
34. B. Samuel Arnold and Edman Spangler
35. D. Samuel J. Seymour
36. C. Freeport, Illinois
37. A. six
38. D. Grandfather
39. C. University of Michigan
40. A. Oneida Community
41. A. law
42. B. Librarian
43. B. Guiteau committed adultery.
44. C. Wisconsin
45. C. evangelist
46. D. John Humphrey Noyes
47. C. *Garfield vs. Hancock*
48. B. Austria or France
49. A. God
50. D. British Bulldog
51. C. dynamite
52. A. Williams College
53. C. "My God, what is that?"
54. D. abdomen
55. A. Willard Bliss
56. D. Unclean hands
57. B. Metal detector
58. D. A and C
59. C. Patrick Kearney
60. D. Confiscate Guiteau's pistol
61. C. "I am a Stalwart of the Stalwarts…Arthur is president now!"
62. B. *The Life and Theology of Charles Guiteau*

63. B. November 14, 1881
64. A. George Scoville
65. A. Elihu Root
66. C. Guiteau was legally insane, and he did not kill Garfield; improper medical care caused his death.
67. C. "You are all low, consummate jackasses!"
68. A. "I am Going to the Lordy"
69. A. Hanging
70. B. syphilis
71. D. They were given to the National Museum of Health and Medicine.
72. D. federally elected officials were guaranteed full-time protection
73. D. Detroit, Michigan
74. A. ten
75. C. Anarchism
76. B. He blamed the president for the nation's economic woes.
77. B. Pan American Exposition in Buffalo, New York / September 6, 1901
78. C. .32 Iver Johnson
79. D. Temple of Music
80. C. Handkerchief
81. A. "Let no one hurt him!"
82. A. Eight days later
83. B. Eight hours
84. B. Electric chair
85. B. Andrew Jackson
86. D. Theodore Roosevelt
87. B. Herbert Hoover
88. C. Giuseppe Zangara
89. B. Al "Scarface" Capone
90. C. Oscar Collazo and Griselio Torresola
91. B. Leslie W. Coffelt
92. C. George Wallace
93. A. Richard Nixon
94. C. "Operation Pandora's Box"
95. B. Lynette Fromme

96. B. Raymond Lee Harvey
97. C. Raymond Donovan
98. B. Two
99. A. Earl David Lee
100. B. Donald Trump

CHAPTER TWO

JOHN F. KENNEDY

1. John Fitzgerald Kennedy (JFK) was born on May 29, 1917, in _____.
   A. Middlebury, Vermont
   B. Newton, Massachusetts
   C. Greenwich, Connecticut
   D. Brookline, Massachusetts

2. The second son of Joseph and Rose Kennedy, he was one of _____ children.
   A. five
   B. nine
   C. eleven
   D. thirteen

3. During his early to middle childhood, JFK was educated at all of the following schools *except* the _____.
   A. Dexter School
   B. Marymount School
   C. Edward Devotion School
   D. Noble and Greenough School

4. Upon completion of his secondary education in 1935, JFK enrolled at _____.
   A. Yale University
   B. Cornell University
   C. Princeton University
   D. Johns Hopkins University

5. The following year, he transferred to Harvard University. While there, he
    excelled at which sport?
    A. Boxing
    B. Rowing
    C. Baseball
    D. Swimming

6. When Joseph Kennedy Sr. was appointed ambassador to Great Britain in
    1938, JFK took a leave of absence from Harvard and traveled to (the) _____.
    A. Germany
    B. Soviet Union
    C. Czechoslovakia
    D. All of the above

7. After he returned to school in September 1939, Kennedy's experiences
    abroad strongly influenced his senior thesis, entitled _____.
    A. "Appeasement in Munich"
    B. "Great Britain as a Naval Power"
    C. "Germany and the Versailles Treaty"
    D. "Catholicism and the Rise of Fascism"

8. The thesis was later published in book form as _____.
    A. *Why England Slept*
    B. *Peace in Our Time*
    C. *At Dawn We Wept*
    D. *Chamberlain's Blunder*

9. Shortly before the Japanese attack on Pearl Harbor, Kennedy joined the
    US Naval Reserve. After completing ROTC training at Northwestern
    University in 1942, he was assigned to which motor torpedo base in the
    South Pacific?
    A. Tulagi
    B. Bellona
    C. Guadalcanal
    D. San Cristobal

10. On August 2, 1943, while operating in enemy waters, JFK's PT boat was cut in half by the Japanese destroyer _____.
    A. *Yanagi*
    B. *Amagiri*
    C. *Okikaze*
    D. *Isokaze*

11. For his heroic efforts to save his crew, Kennedy was awarded which noncombat decoration?
    A. Defense Service Medal
    B. Navy Achievement Medal
    C. Distinguished Service Medal
    D. Navy and Marine Corps Medal

12. Returning home in 1945, JFK secured a temporary position as a _____.
    A. bank teller
    B. history teacher
    C. radio announcer
    D. newspaper reporter

13. With the death of Joseph Kennedy Jr. in World War II, it became JFK's "responsibility" to pursue a career in politics. Who made that decision?
    A. Rose Kennedy
    B. Eunice Kennedy
    C. Bobby Kennedy
    D. Joseph Kennedy Sr.

14. How many challengers did young Kennedy face in his first Congressional primary in 1946?
    A. Five
    B. Nine
    C. Eleven
    D. Twelve

15. By which percentage of the vote did JFK win the general election?
    A. 49.7
    B. 58.2
    C. 61.9
    D. 71.8

16. After spending six uneventful years in the House of Representatives, JFK ran for the US Senate, defeating this formidable incumbent.
    A. Joseph Russo
    B. Michael Neville
    C. Francis Rooney
    D. Henry Cabot Lodge Jr.

17. Who was the future US Speaker of the House that subsequently filled Kennedy's congressional seat?
    A. Carl Albert
    B. Tip O'Neill
    C. Sam Rayburn
    D. John McCormick

18. On September 12, 1953, JFK married socialite Jacqueline Lee Bouvier. For which newspaper did she work as a photojournalist?
    A. *The New York Times*
    B. *The Washington Post*
    C. *The Philadelphia Bulletin*
    D. *The Washington Times-Herald*

19. At the 1956 Democratic National Convention, Kennedy nearly became Adlai Stevenson's vice presidential running mate. To whom did he lose the nomination?
    A. Senator John Stennis
    B. Senator Wayne Morse
    C. Senator Estes Kefauver
    D. Senator James Eastland

20. In 1957, JFK was awarded the Pulitzer Prize for _____, a volume containing short biographies of eight heroic US senators.
    A. *The Last Hurrah*
    B. *Profiles in Courage*
    C. *Ruffles and Flourishes*
    D. *The Making of the President*

21. Which Kennedy aide allegedly helped research and write the book?
    A. Robert Wallace
    B. McGeorge Bundy
    C. Theodore Sorensen
    D. Anthony Celebrezze

22. On January 2, 1960, JFK declared his candidacy for president. Where did he make the announcement?
    A. Washington, DC
    B. Detroit, Michigan
    C. Salt Lake City, Utah
    D. Boston, Massachusetts

23. Which of the following US senators challenged Kennedy for the Democratic Party's nomination?
    A. John Iselin
    B. George Smathers
    C. J. William Fulbright
    D. None of the above

24. On July 11–15, 1960, the Democratic National Convention was held in _____.
    A. Miami, Florida
    B. Cleveland, Ohio
    C. Los Angeles, California
    D. Pittsburgh, Pennsylvania

25. Which of these US senators was *not* considered as a possible vice-presidential running mate by JFK?
    A. Carl Hayden
    B. Thomas Jordan
    C. Stuart Symington
    D. Hubert Humphrey

26. In the end, Kennedy selected Senator Lyndon Johnson to share the ticket. Why?
    A. He owed Johnson several political favors.
    B. As a Southerner, Johnson would balance the ticket.
    C. Johnson had always dreamed of being vice president.
    D. It was the best way to prevent Johnson from challenging him in 1964.

27. By what percentage of the vote did JFK secure his party's nomination?
    A. 52.8
    B. 55.7
    C. 57.5
    D. 59.1

28. On September 26, 1960, Kennedy faced his Republican opponent, Vice President Richard Nixon, in the first of four televised debates. On which network and in which city did the debate take place?
    A. CBS / Chicago
    B. ABC / New York
    C. PBS / Los Angeles
    D. NBC / San Francisco

29. The majority of those who watched the debate on TV felt that _____.
    A. JFK had won
    B. Nixon had won
    C. both candidates did well
    D. neither candidate did well

30. Of the people who listened on the radio, the majority thought that _____.
    A. JFK had won
    B. Nixon had won
    C. both candidates did well
    D. neither candidate did well

31. In one of the closest elections in presidential history, JFK defeated Nixon by fewer than _____.
    A. 85,00 popular votes
    B. 95,00 popular votes
    C. 100,000 popular votes
    D. 120,000 popular votes

32. Less than a month after the election, a retired postal worker plotted to assassinate President-elect Kennedy in Palm Beach, Florida. However, at the last minute, he changed his mind. What was his name?
    A. James Elliot Tudeski
    B. Richard Paul Pavlick
    C. Karl Michael Howard
    D. George Henry Bowen

33. On January 20, 1961, JFK was sworn into office as the thirty-fifth president of the United States by which member of the Supreme Court?
    A. Hugo Black
    B. Earl Warren
    C. Potter Stewart
    D. Warren Burger

34. All the following held positions in the new administration *except* _____.
    A. Clark Clifford
    B. Stewart Udall
    C. William Wirtz
    D. Luther Hodges

35. In addition to his formal cabinet, Kennedy surrounded himself with an informal group of loyalists known as the _____.
    A. "Irish Mafia"
    B. "Papal Mafia"
    C. "Boston Mafia"
    D. "Harvard Mafia"

36. JFK was the first US president to conduct live televised press conferences. How many were held during his 1,063 days in office?
    A. Sixty-four
    B. Sixty-seven
    C. Seventy-one
    D. Seventy-five

37. All of these were key foreign policy issues between 1961 and 1963 *except* _____.
    A. Bay of Pigs
    B. U-2 Incident
    C. Vietnam War
    D. Cuban Missile Crisis

38. In which order did these civil rights episodes occur?
    1. Civil rights activist Medgar Evers was assassinated.
    2. Freedom Riders were attacked in Birmingham, Alabama.
    3. James Meredith gained admission to the University of Mississippi.
    4. Governor George Wallace banned Black people from attending the University of Alabama.
    A. 2., 3., 4., 1.
    B. 1., 2., 4., 3.
    C. 4., 2., 1., 3.
    D. 3., 1., 2., 4.

39. Early in 1963, JFK began planning his reelection campaign. In which region of the country did he anticipate strong opposition?
    A. East
    B West
    C. North
    D. South

40. In the late spring, Kennedy announced that he would visit Texas in November. Why?
    A. To celebrate the 120th anniversary of Texas statehood
    B. To mend differences between competing elements in the Democratic Party
    C. To raise money for Senator John Tower's reelection campaign
    D. To mediate a dispute between Governor John Connally and Senator William Blakeley

41. Coordinating security for the trip was the responsibility of which Secret Service agent(s)?
    A. Roy Kellerman
    B. Forrest Sorrels
    C. Winston Lawson
    D. A and B

42. Who was the White House "advance man" that planned the president's Texas itinerary?
    A. Jerry Bruno
    B. Michael Banatos
    C. Timothy Reardon
    D. Brendan Mitchell

43. On November 21, 1963, JFK began his five-city swing through "The Lone Star State" with a stopover in San Antonio, where he dedicated the School of Aerospace Medicine at _____.
    A. Brooks Air Force Base
    B. Carswell Air Force Base
    C. McConnell Air Force Base
    D. Vandenberg Air Force Base

44. Later that day, the president and first lady attended a testimonial dinner for US Congressman _____ in Houston.
    A. Jack Brooks
    B. Robert Casey
    C. Albert Thomas
    D. Henry Gonzalez

45. In the evening, the Kennedys flew to Fort Worth. At which hotel did they stay?
    A. Hotel Texas
    B. Wells Fargo Inn
    C. Sam Houston Plaza
    D. Fort Worth Regency

46. The next morning, November 22, JFK was the guest of honor at a Fort Worth Chamber of Commerce event, where he received a _____.
    A. saddle and chaps
    B. horse and wagon
    C. fishing rod and reel
    D. cowboy hat and boots

47. Before departing for Dallas, Kennedy allegedly made which prophetic statement?[9]
    A. "The president is vulnerable when he is out amongst a large crowd of people."
    B. "If anyone was crazy enough to kill the president, all they had to do was shoot at him from a distance."
    C. "If somebody wants to shoot me from a window with a rifle, nobody can stop it, so why worry about it?"
    D. "Someday an assassin will shoot the president in his limousine like Archduke Franz Ferdinand in 1914."

48. Following a brief thirteen-minute flight to "Big D," *Air Force One* landed at
    _____.
    A. Love Field
    B. Alamo Airport
    C. Dallas Municipal Field
    D. Johnson National Airport

49. On the tarmac, the Kennedys were welcomed by Mayor Earle Cabell and other city dignitaries. Which gift did Mrs. Cabell present to the first lady?
    A. Box of candy
    B. Solid-gold key
    C. Bouquet of red roses
    D. Heart-shaped bracelet

50. After greeting an enthusiastic crowd that had gathered along the airport fence line, the Kennedys and Governor and Mrs. John Connally took their places in the presidential limousine. According to the schedule arranged by the Secret Service and Dallas Police, the motorcade was to exit the airport and turn left on Mockingbird Lane, then right on Lemmon Avenue toward Cedar Springs Road. From there, it would follow Cedar Springs to Harwood Street into the downtown area. The motorcade would then turn onto Main Street from Harwood before arriving in Dealey Plaza, where it would turn right on Houston Street and left on Elm Street to reach the access road to Stemmons Freeway. How many minutes were allotted for the estimated ten-mile trip?
    A. Fifteen
    B. Twenty-five
    C. Forty-five
    D. Seventy-five

51. Following the motorcade, JFK's only official engagement before flying to Austin was a luncheon hosted by members of the local business community. Where was the event to be held?
    A. Trade Mart
    B. Market Hall
    C. North Star Pavilion
    D. Cattlemen's Annex

52. In which Dallas newspapers were details of the parade route published seventy-two hours earlier on November 19?
    A. *Daily Herald* and *Globe News*
    B. *Morning News* and *Times-Herald*
    C. *Southern Gazette* and *Daily Times*
    D. *Times-Dispatch* and *Courier-Journal*

53. Who was the high-ranking Dallas Police official in charge of traffic control that day?
   A. Chief Jesse Curry
   B. Lieutenant Trevor Atkins
   C. Captain Perdue Lawrence
   D. Deputy Chief George Lumpkin

54. Name the veteran Secret Service agent who drove the specially designed presidential touring car (SS-100-X)? He was also the oldest member of JFK's security detail.
   A. David Grant
   B. Stewart Stout
   C. William Greer
   D. Roy Kellerman

55. Located directly behind SS-100-X was the Secret Service follow-up car: a 1955 Cadillac convertible. Code named "Halfback," it was unofficially dubbed (the) _____ by the White House press corps.
   A. "Big Bertha"
   B. "Old Smokey"
   C. "Queen Mary"
   D. "Mean Machine"

56. Including automobiles, police motorcycles, and buses, what was the total number of vehicles taking part in the motorcade?
   A. Thirty-two
   B. Forty-eight
   C. Sixty-seven
   D. Eighty-four

57. As the presidential party traveled through the suburbs of Dallas, JFK noticed a group of school-age children holding a banner. What did it say?
   A. "STOP MR. KENNEDY, WE LOVE YOU!"
   B. "PLEASE STOP AND SHAKE OUR HANDS!"
   C. "MR. PRESIDENT, STOP AND HAVE LUNCH!"
   D. "PLEASE STOP AND WISH ME HAPPY BIRTHDAY!"

58. In all, how many unscheduled stops were made along the route?
   A. One
   B. Two
   C. Four
   D. Seven

59. When the presidential caravan reached the downtown area, the crowds were large and friendly, except for those individuals holding protest signs and distributing flyers that read _____.
   A. "Wanted for Treason"
   B. "Mr. President, Go Back to Russia"
   C. "Communist Go Back to Washington"
   D. "Help Kennedy Stamp Out Democracy"

60. At 12:29 p.m., the motorcade arrived in Dealey Plaza. As SS-X-100 passed the Texas School Book Depository (TSBD), a nondescript seven-story building on Elm Street, rifle fire rang out. Which of the following is the likely sequence of events?
   1. One shot misses President Kennedy.
   2. One shot strikes President Kennedy in the head.
   3. One shot wounds President Kennedy then Governor Connally.
   A. 3., 1., 2.
   B. 1., 3., 2.
   C. 2., 1., 3.
   D. 3., 2., 1.

61. How fast was the presidential limousine moving between the first and third shots?
    A. 10.6 mph
    B. 11.2 mph
    C. 13.5 mph
    D. 14.9 mph

62. Ironically, what had Mrs. Connally said to JFK moments earlier?[10]
    A. "Mr. President, we are proud to be Texans."
    B. "Mr. President, you can't say Dallas doesn't love you."
    C. "Mr. President, isn't it a wonderful day to be in Texas?"
    D. "Mr. President, you're certainly getting a wonderful reception."

63. Name the Secret Service agent who made a gallant but futile attempt to shield the president and first lady from the gunfire.
    A. Clint Hill
    B. Paul Landis
    C. John Ready
    D. William McIntyre

64. Who was the eyewitness "wounded" during the shooting?
    A. Lee Bowers
    B. James Tague
    C. Frances Moffit
    D. Howard Brennan

65. How many amateur photographers were filming in or near Dealey Plaza?
    A. Five
    B. Seven
    C. Eleven
    D. Thirteen

66. Who was the only person to capture the assassination in its entirety with his / her Bell & Howell Director Series Zoomatic Camera Model 414PD with Kodachrome II eight-millimeter film and a Varamat telephoto lens?
    A. Tina Towner
    B. Charles Bronson
    C. Marie Muchmore
    D. Abraham Zapruder

67. Following the third shot, the presidential limousine raced the short distance to Parkland Memorial Hospital via which major highway?
    A. Rayburn Drive
    B. Stemmons Freeway
    C. Will Travis Boulevard
    D. Longacre Expressway

68. Arriving at 12:35 p.m., Kennedy and Connally were registered as patient _____ and _____, respectively.
    A. 24740 / 24743
    B. 25610 / 25611
    C. 27830 / 27832
    D. 29690 / 29691

69. Who was the English-born nurse that removed the president's blood-soaked clothing in Trauma Room One?
    A. Kim Hoover
    B. Diana Bowron
    C. Victoria Simpkiss
    D. Constance Conners

70. A senior surgical resident, he was the first physician to treat JFK.
    A. Red Duke
    B. Evan Mueller
    C. Trevor Baxter
    D. Charles Carrico

71. Which medical procedure was initially performed on the president?
    A. Spinal tap
    B. Tracheotomy
    C. Cardiac massage
    D. Blood transfusion

72. In total, how many doctors and nurses assisted in JFK's treatment?
    A. Eleven
    B. Twelve
    C. Fifteen
    D. Thirty

73. When all lifesaving measures proved ineffective, the chief of neurosurgery pronounced the president dead at 1:00 p.m. What was his name?
    A. Kemp Clark
    B. Paul Withers
    C. Malcolm Perry
    D. Robert McClelland

74. At 1:32 p.m., UPI announced that Oscar Huber, the pastor of Holy Trinity Catholic Church in Dallas, had administered the last rites to JFK. Who was the priest that accompanied Huber?
    A. Reverend Patrick R. O'Brien
    B. Monsignor Robert F. Stewart
    C. Reverend James N. Thompson
    D. Monsignor Albert A. Delmonico

75. Leaving the hospital, what did Reverend Huber allegedly say to reporters? It was a statement that he would later categorically deny.[11]
    A. "He's dead, all right!"
    B. "I can't believe he's gone!"
    C. "They've killed our president!"
    D. "Our beloved president is dead!"

76. Name the White House deputy press secretary who made the official announcement that President Kennedy had died.
    A. Pierre Salinger
    B. Malcolm Kilduff
    C. Andrew Hatcher
    D. William Brennan

77. Which CBS soap opera was preempted by news of the events in Dallas?
    A. *Days of Our Lives*
    B. *The Edge of Night*
    C. *As the World Turns*
    D. *Search for Tomorrow*

78. "The most trusted man in America," he was the legendary anchorman who fought back tears announcing JFK's death.
    A. Eric Sevareid
    B. Walter Cronkite
    C. Edward R. Murrow
    D. John Cameron Swayze

79. In the confusion that occurred immediately after the assassination, the news media erroneously reported all the following *except* _____.
    A. the sniper fired from the fifth-floor window of the TSBD
    B. after searching the TSBD, Dallas Police found no weapon
    C. Vice President Johnson suffered a stroke en route to the hospital
    D. the fatal wound inflicted on the president entered at the base of the throat

80. Because the president's murder had occurred in Texas, and there was no federal law prohibiting such a crime, the Dallas County coroner tried (unsuccessfully) to prevent the removal of JFK's body from Parkland Hospital. What was his name?
    A. Earl Rose
    B. Lester Wolff
    C. Gustav Peabody
    D. Carson Simones

81. Once the casket bearing the thirty-fifth president was aboard *Air Force One*, Vice President Lyndon Johnson was sworn in as the thirty-sixth president of the United States. Which federal judge administered the oath of office?
A. Lynn F. Myers
B. Sara T. Hughes
C. Rebecca D. Doyle
D. Judy H. Sheindlin

82. How many people were present for the historic swearing-in ceremony on *Air Force One*?
A. Nine
B. Fifteen
C. Eighteen
D. Twenty-six

83. On the flight back to Andrews Air Force Base, it was decided that the president's autopsy should be performed at the National Naval Medical Center (Bethesda Naval Hospital). Who made the decision and why?
A. Lyndon Johnson / It was required by federal law.
B. J. Edgar Hoover / Walter Reed Army Hospital was not available.
C. Dwight Eisenhower / It was the official hospital for US presidents.
D. Jacqueline Kennedy / JFK had served in the US Navy during World War II.

84. In addition to Jacqueline Kennedy, which other member of the Kennedy family accompanied JFK's body to Bethesda Hospital?
A. Rose Kennedy
B. Ethel Kennedy
C. Robert Kennedy
D. Edward Kennedy

85. Of the following military pathologists, which one did *not* participate in the postmortem?
    A. Major Bennett Marco, USA
    B. Commander James Humes, USN
    C. Lieutenant Colonel Pierre Finck, USA
    D. Commander J. Thornton Boswell, USN

86. Who were the members of the medical staff that took the color and black-and-white photographs during the autopsy?
    A. John Stringer and Floyd Riebe
    B. Edward Reed and Jerrol Custer
    C. William Pitzer and John Ebersole
    D. Paul O'Connor and James Jenkins

87. A Washington, DC, landmark for more than one hundred years, it was the mortuary that prepared the president's remains for burial.
    A. Frazier Mason
    B. Everly-Wheatley
    C. Pinckney-Spangler
    D. Joseph Gawler's Sons

88. Name the commanding general of the Military District of Washington charged with planning JFK's state funeral.
    A. John B. Cole, USAF
    B. Philip C. Wehle, USA
    C. Edwin X. Marshall, USMC
    D. Harry H. Bandholtz, USA

89. At the request of Mrs. Kennedy, elements of the ceremony were modeled after those of which former US president?
    A. James Garfield
    B. Abraham Lincoln
    C. William McKinley
    D. George Washington

90. Who were the two Catholic University priests that remained with the president's body until the funeral?
A. Monsignor Robert Mohan and Reverend Gilbert Hartke
B. Reverend Nobert Thomas and Monsignor Karl Mitchner
C. Monsignor William Norris and Reverend Robert Simone
D. Reverend Mitchell Webster and Monsignor Tyler Rogers

91. At the public viewing in the Rotunda of the US Capitol, all of the following officials eulogized JFK *except* _____.
A. Congressman Ira Peck
B. Senator Mike Mansfield
C. Chief Justice Earl Warren
D. Speaker of the House John McCormick

92. In which Washington cathedral was the funeral service held?
A. St. John the Baptist
B. Chapel of the Holy Cross
C. St. Matthew the Apostle
D. Basilica of the Immaculate Conception

93. Who was the archbishop of Boston and friend of the Kennedy family that celebrated the mass?
A. Cardinal Patrick O'Boyle
B. Cardinal James McIntyre
C. Cardinal Richard Cushing
D. Cardinal Francis Spellman

94. Name the Catholic priest who narrated the proceedings for the worldwide TV and radio audience from the basement of the cathedral.
A. Bishop William Hooper
B. Cardinal Joseph Mitchell
C. Reverend Michael Thomas
D. Monsignor Leonard Hurley

95. How many foreign dignitaries traveled to Washington, DC, to pay their respects?
    A. 31
    B. 89
    C. 150
    D. 220

96. Who was the English-born movie star that attended the funeral?
    A. Sean Connery
    B. Michael Caine
    C. Peter Lawford
    D. Richard Burton

97. Standing 15.1 hands and weighing nearly 1,200 pounds, it was the caparisoned or "riderless" horse that followed JFK's caisson to Arlington National Cemetery.
    A. "Black Jack"
    B. "Man o' War"
    C. "War Admiral"
    D. "Sergeant York"

98. Which European military unit participated in the burial service?
    A. Welsh Marines
    B. Royal Scots Greys
    C. Irish Army Cadets
    D. French Foreign Legion

99. By a cruel twist of fate, whose birthday was on the same day that JFK was buried?
    A. Patrick Kennedy
    B. Caroline Kennedy
    C. John F. Kennedy Jr.
    D. Jacqueline Kennedy

100. Prior to the assassination of John F. Kennedy, which of the following events was considered the "Crime of the Century"?
A. Great Train Robbery
B. Lindbergh Kidnapping
C. Teapot Dome Scandal
D. St. Valentine's Day Massacre

CHAPTER TWO ANSWERS

1. D. Brookline, Massachusetts
2. B. nine
3. B. Marymount School
4. C. Princeton University
5. D. Swimming
6. D. All of the above
7. A. "Appeasement in Munich"
8. A. *Why England Slept*
9. A. Tulagi
10. B. *Amagiri*
11. D. Navy and Marine Corps Medal
12. D. newspaper reporter
13. D. Joseph Kennedy Sr.
14. B. Nine
15. A. 49.7
16. D. Henry Cabot Lodge Jr.
17. B. Tip O'Neill
18. D. *The Washington Times-Herald*
19. C. Senator Estes Kefauver
20. B. *Profiles in Courage*
21. C. Theodore Sorensen
22. A. Washington, DC
23. D. None of the above
24. C. Los Angeles, California
25. A. Carl Hayden
26. B. As a Southerner, Johnson would balance the ticket.
27. A. 52.8
28. A. CBS / Chicago
29. A. JFK had won
30. B. Nixon had won

31. D. 120,000 popular votes
32. B. Richard Paul Pavlick
33. B. Earl Warren
34. A. Clark Clifford
35. A. "Irish Mafia"
36. A. Sixty-four
37. B. U-2 Incident
38. A. 2., 3., 4., 1.
39. D. South
40. B. To mend differences between competing elements in the Democratic Party
41. D. A and B
42. A. Jerry Bruno
43. A. Brooks Air Force Base
44. C. Albert Thomas
45. A. Hotel Texas
46. D. cowboy hat and boots
47. C. "If somebody wants to shoot me from a window with a rifle, nobody can stop it, so why worry about it?"
48. A. Love Field
49. C. Bouquet of red roses
50. D. Forty-five
51. A. Trade Mart
52. B. *Morning News* and *Times-Herald*
53. B. Captain Perdue Lawrence
54. C. William Greer
55. C. "Queen Mary"
56. B. Forty-eight
57. B. "PLEASE STOP AND SHAKE OUR HANDS!"
58. B. Two
59. A. "Wanted for Treason"
60. B. 1., 3., 2.
61. B. 11.2 mph

62. B. "Mr. President, you can't say Dallas doesn't love you."
63. A. Clint Hill
64. B. James Tague
65. D. Thirteen
66. D. Abraham Zapruder
67. B. Stemmons Freeway
68. A. 24740 / 24743
69. B. Diana Bowron
70. D. Charles Carrico
71. B. Tracheotomy
72. D. Thirty
73. A. Kemp Clark
74. C. Reverend James N. Thompson
75. A. "He's dead, all right!"
76. B. Malcolm Kilduff
77. C. *As the World Turns*
78. B. Walter Cronkite
79. C. Vice President Johnson suffered a stroke en route to the hospital
80. A. Earl Rose
81. B. Sara T. Hughes
82. D. Twenty-six
83. D. Jacqueline Kennedy / JFK had served in the US Navy during World War II.
84. C. Robert Kennedy
85. A. Major Bennett Marco, USA
86. A. John Stringer and Floyd Riebe
87. D. Joseph Gawler's Sons
88. B. Philip C. Wehle, USA
89. B. Abraham Lincoln
90. A. Monsignor Robert Mohan and Reverend Gilbert Hartke
91. A. Congressman Ira Peck
92. C. St. Matthew the Apostle
93. C. Cardinal Richard Cushing
94. D. Monsignor Leonard Hurley

95. D. 220
96. C. Peter Lawford
97. A. "Black Jack"
98. C. Irish Army Cadets
99. C. John F. Kennedy Jr.
100. B. Lindbergh Kidnapping

CHAPTER THREE

LEE HARVEY OSWALD

1. Lee Harvey Oswald was born on October 18, 1939, in _____.
   A. Denver, Colorado
   B. Louisville, Kentucky
   C. Knoxville, Tennessee
   D. New Orleans, Louisiana

2. Two months prior to his birth, Oswald's father Robert died of (a) _____.
   A. lung cancer
   B. heart attack
   C. pneumonia
   D. gunshot wound

3. Oswald was the third of _____ children.
   A. three
   B. seven
   C. eleven
   D. None of the above

4. In 1942, he and his older brothers were placed in which of the following orphanages by their mother, Marguerite?
   A. St. Vincent's Home
   B. Mercy Boy's Ranch
   C. Bethlehem Children's Home
   D. The Baptist Home for Children

5. After two years in the facility, the boys were withdrawn, and the family moved to _____.
   A. Dallas, Texas
   B. Macon, Georgia
   C. Brownsville, Texas
   D. Athens, Tennessee

6. In 1945, Marguerite married businessman _____.
   A. Joseph Nye
   B. Edwin Ekdahl
   C. Simon Peterman
   D. Clarence Summerville

7. Due to irreconcilable differences, the couple divorced in _____.
   A. 1946
   B. 1947
   C. 1948
   D. 1949

8. At the age of thirteen, Oswald and his mother moved to New York. Enrolled in P.S. 117, he was truant a total of _____.
   A. fifteen days
   B. thirty-two days
   C. forty-seven days
   D. seventy-five days

9. When not attending school, Oswald would often visit the _____.
   A. Bronx Zoo
   B. Statue of Liberty
   C. Empire State Building
   D. Metropolitan Museum of Art

10. Because of behavioral issues, Oswald was remanded to which of the
    following detention homes?
    A. Smith House
    B. Milmont Hall
    C. Bedford Children's Village
    D. Chase County Correctional Center

11. While he was at the facility, it was determined by psychologist Irving
    Sokolow that Oswald possessed an IQ of _____.
    A. 101
    B. 118
    C. 126
    D. 150

12. Oswald first became interested in politics after reading a leaflet about the
    execution(s) of _____.
    A. Fred and Ethel Mertz
    B. Bruno Richard Hauptmann
    C. Julius and Ethel Rosenberg
    D. Nicola Sacco and Bartolomeo Vanzetti

13. At the age of fifteen, Oswald began studying which of the following
    ideologies?
    A. Fascism
    B. Socialism
    C. Liberalism
    D. Communism

14. Eventually, Oswald and his mother left New York and relocated to _____.
    A. Austin, Texas
    B. Flagstaff, Arizona
    C. New Orleans, Louisiana
    D. Farmington, New Mexico

15. Which youth organization did Oswald join in 1955?
    A. Boy Scouts
    B. Young Democrats
    C. Student Model Congress
    D. None of the above

16. On October 24, 1956, Oswald enlisted in the US Marine Corps. Why?
    A. He had been drafted.
    B. His father had been a Marine.
    C. He wanted to travel the world.
    D. His mother was too controlling.

17. During basic training, which rating did he achieve on the rifle range?
    A. Expert
    B. Marksman
    C. Unqualified
    D. Sharpshooter

18. Following boot camp, Oswald was assigned to Camp Pendleton,
    California, and later to Keesler Air Force Base in Biloxi, Mississippi, where
    he qualified as a(n) _____.
    A. radar operator
    B. fire control technician
    C. heavy weapons specialist
    D. aviation electronics operator

19. When he was subsequently stationed at Atsugi Air Base in Japan, his unit's
    designation was _____.
    A. Marine Air Group Two
    B. Marine Task Force Four
    C. Marine Air Control Squadron One
    D. Marine Ground Control Unit Eight

20. In his spare time, Oswald tried to learn which of the following languages?
    A. French
    B. German
    C. Russian
    D. Chinese

21. Considered peculiar by fellow Marines, Oswald was nicknamed _____.
    A. "Frenchy"
    B. "Sauerkraut"
    C. "Oswaldskovich"
    D. "Comrade Oswald"

22. Less than three years after joining the Marines, Oswald received a hardship discharge. Why?
    A. He claimed that his mother was ill.
    B. He claimed that his sister had died.
    C. He claimed that his brother was ill.
    D. He claimed that his father had died.

23. Although Oswald had decided to defect to the Soviet Union, which reason did he give US passport officials for traveling abroad?
    A. He wanted to tour World War I battlefields in France.
    B. He wanted to visit the Great Pyramids of Giza in Egypt.
    C. He wanted to attend the wedding of his cousin in Germany.
    D. He wanted to enroll at Albert Schweitzer College in Switzerland.

24. On October 16, 1959, Oswald arrived in Moscow by way of the United Kingdom and Finland. How was he able afford his trip?
    A. He won $900 playing poker.
    B. He supposedly borrowed $1,000 from his mother.
    C. He allegedly saved $1,500 from his Marine Corps salary.
    D. He obtained a $2,000 loan from a bank in Fort Worth, Texas.

25. When Soviet officials told Oswald that he could not remain in the country, how did he react?
    A. He slashed his wrist.
    B. He shot himself in the foot.
    C. He jumped in front of a bus.
    D. He overdosed on sleeping pills.

26. After recovering in a Moscow hospital, Oswald informed the American embassy that he _____.
    A. wanted to travel to Cuba
    B. wanted to return to the US
    C. wanted to defect to Russia
    D. wanted to join the Soviet army

27. Uncertain of Oswald's motives, authorities sent the American to the city of Minsk and placed him under surveillance. Which of the following was his KGB file number?
    A. 18268
    B. 20896
    C. 31451
    D. 46823

28. Who was the Russian defector who later claimed to have knowledge of Oswald's activities in the Soviet Union?
    A. Yuri Nosenko
    B. Alexei Titovits
    C. Igor Danilovich
    D. Vladimir Pushkin

29. In Minsk, he found employment as a metalworker at the _____.
    A. Novatek Steel Works
    B. Rostec Munitions Plant
    C. Aeroflot Tractor Company
    D. Gorizont Electronics Factory

30. Shortly after his defection, Oswald was interviewed by two American journalists. Who were they?
    A. Ethel Payne and Lara Logan
    B. Amy Kaufman and Denise Curry
    C. Priscilla Johnson and Aline Mosby
    D. Barbara Tuchman and Doris Kearns

31. While at a trade union dance, Oswald met his future wife, _____.
    A. Marina Lebedev
    B. Marina Morozov
    C. Marina Prusakova
    D. Marina Yurchenko

32. After the death of her mother, Marina moved to Minsk to live with her aunt and uncle, who was a colonel with this Soviet agency.
    A. Bureau of Agriculture
    B. Ministry of Internal Affairs
    C. Bureau of International Security
    D. Ministry of Military Procurement

33. Which of the following was Marina's occupation?
    A. Supermarket clerk
    B. Pharmacy student
    C. Elementary school teacher
    D. Insurance company secretary

34. How long did Oswald and Marina date before marrying?
    A. Two days
    B. Seven weeks
    C. More than a year
    D. Less than six weeks

35. To whom did Oswald propose marriage prior to Marina?
    A. Irina Kuzmich
    B. Ella Germann
    C. Roza Kuznetsova
    D. Valentina Timenshekov

36. By 1961, Oswald was becoming disillusioned with the Russian lifestyle because _____.
    A. the winters were too cold
    B. work at the factory was boring
    C. he was not earning enough money
    D. All of the above

37. With which American embassy official did Oswald meet to discuss his return to the US?
    A. Richard Snyder
    B. George Schallert
    C. Broderick Meyers
    D. Wallace Mitchum

38. After having his passport reinstated and receiving an exit visa, Oswald and Marina traveled by train to Rotterdam, where they boarded the SS *Maasdam* for the return trip to America. When they arrived at the Fifth Street pier in Hoboken, New Jersey, on June 13, 1962, they were met by a case worker with the Traveler's Aid Society. What was his name?
    A. Spas T. Raikin
    B. Petar R. Hitov
    C. Filip L. Dimitar
    D. Georgi G. Karev

39. Settling in the Fort Worth / Dallas area, Oswald befriended a Russian émigré named _____. On March 29, 1977, he told author Edward J. Epstein that he had monitored Oswald for the CIA. That same day, he committed suicide.
    A. Igor Dorenski
    B. Victor Crenskev
    C. Vladimir Sempkorol
    D. George de Morenschildt

40. In January 1963, Oswald mail ordered a handgun bearing serial number V510210 from _____ for _____.
    A. Guns and Things of Knoxville, Tennessee / $30.00
    B. Seaport Traders of Los Angeles, California / $29.95
    C. Miller's Hunting Company, Kenosha, Wisconsin / $19.95
    D. Long Island Gun Emporium of Albany, New York / $28.50

41. On March 4, 1963, Marina Oswald was placed under FBI surveillance. Which agent was assigned to her case?
    A. William Depuy
    B. Richard Kramer
    C. Gordon Shanklin
    D. None of the above

42. Less than two weeks later, Oswald ordered a 6.5 Mannlicher-Carcano rifle bearing serial number C7266 and a telescopic sight from (the) _____.
    A. Miller's Gun Shop of Provo, Utah
    B. Bradley Gun Barn of Cleveland, Ohio
    C. Klein's Sporting Goods of Chicago, Illinois
    D. Sportsman's Mart of Pittsburgh, Pennsylvania

43. Which alias did Oswald use to make the purchase?
    A. O. H. Lee
    B. A. Hidell
    C. O. L. Harvey
    D. Lee Osborne

44. How much did both items cost?
    A. $10.69
    B. $19.95
    C. $37.68
    D. $46.70

45. Oswald would later be photographed with the rifle, pistol, and two left-wing newspapers. Who reportedly took the pictures?
    A. John Pickford
    B. Marina Oswald
    C. Edward Mitchell
    D. Marguerite Oswald

46. Which type of camera was used?
    A. Traid Fotront
    B. Karon Marquis
    C. Braun Gloriette
    D. Imperial Reflex

47. On April 10, 1963, Oswald tried unsuccessfully to shoot right-wing US general _____.
    A. Walter Kelly
    B. Joseph Stiller
    C. Edwin Walker
    D. Albert Mitchell

48. Shortly after the botched assassination attempt, he moved his family to New Orleans where he found employment at the _____.
    A. Hauser Arboretum
    B. Reily Coffee Company
    C. Unity Savings and Loan
    D. RGX Electronics Company

49. In the "Big Easy," Oswald's interest in politics continued when he opened his own chapter of the _____.
    A. Committee for Cuban Affairs
    B. Fair Play for Cuba Committee
    C. Committee for Cuban Fair Play
    D. Fair Play Committee for Cubans

50. The organization's national membership included such prominent American writers as Norman Mailer, James Baldwin, and _____.
    A. George Orwell
    B. John Steinbeck
    C. Truman Capote
    D. William Faulkner

51. While distributing propaganda leaflets in downtown New Orleans on August 9, 1963, Oswald scuffled with this anti-Castro activist.
    A. Oscar Tamayo
    B. Manuel Ortega
    C. Hiram Martinez
    D. Carlos Bringuier

52. On which radio show did Oswald later debate the Cuban exile?
    A. *Viva America*
    B. *The Latin Perspective*
    C. *Puerto Rican Panorama*
    D. *Conversation Carte Blanche*

53. Less than two months before the assassination, Oswald traveled by bus to ____.
    A. Quebec, Canada
    B. Monterrey, Mexico
    C. Edmonton, Canada
    D. Mexico City, Mexico

54. Arriving on September 27, 1963, he visited the Cuban consulate, where he tried to obtain permission to visit the country. Why?
    A. He wanted to meet Fidel Castro.
    B. He wanted to do some sightseeing.
    C. He wanted to attend Havana University.
    D. He wanted to become a guerrilla fighter.

55. Oswald also appeared at the Soviet embassy, where he met with which of the following KGB officers?
    A. Maxim Litnov and Eduard Vyshinsky
    B. Valery Kostikov and Oleg Nechiporenko
    C. Nikolai Konstanov and Leonid Nikolayev
    D. Sergey Pitinetsky and Vladimir Mikhailov

56. Unsuccessful in his attempt to enter Cuba, Oswald returned to the US and joined Marina in Dallas, where she was living with her friend, Ruth Paine. It was Paine who suggested that Oswald apply for work at the TSBD. Who was the building superintendent that offered Oswald a job?
    A. Roy Truly
    B. Allen Melvin
    C. Lester Walker
    D. Harold Myers

57. The day before Oswald was hired, he rented a room in the Dallas neighborhood of Oak Cliff. Who was his landlady / housekeeper?
    A. Doris Stevens
    B. Myrtle Jeffries
    C. Earlene Roberts
    D. Mildred Samuels

58. On October 16, Oswald began work at the TSBD filling orders for which book publisher?
    A. Doubleday
    B. McGraw-Hill
    C. Random House
    D. Scott-Foresman

59. How much did the job pay?
    A. $1.00 an hour
    B. $1.15 an hour
    C. $1.20 an hour
    D. $1.25 an hour

60. On the evening before the assassination, Oswald stayed with Marina at Ruth Paine's house. The next morning, before going to work, he left two items on the dresser. What were they?
    A. Cigarette lighter and a rabbit's foot
    B. Pocket knife and his bank statement
    C. Love letter to Marina and a yellow rose
    D. Wedding ring and his wallet containing $170

61. Oswald then proceeded to the garage where he retrieved a package wrapped in brown paper and placed it in the backseat of the car. What did he later tell police the package contained?
    A. Pool cues
    B. Curtain rods
    C. Pieces of wood
    D. Fishing rod and reel

62. Who was the TSBD employee that drove Oswald to work that morning?
    A. Billy Ray Frazier
    B. Bobby Joe Frazier
    C. Buell Wesley Frazier
    D. Bufford Rhea Frazier

63. How many minutes before the assassination was Oswald observed on the sixth floor of the TSBD?
    A. Five
    B. Three
    C. Seven
    D. Thirty

64. Name the Oswald "look-alike" who was standing in the doorway of the TSBD at the time of the assassination.
    A. Billy Lovelady
    B. Wilbert Myers
    C. Raymond Shaw
    D. Jack Dougherty

65. The subject of Barry Ernest's *The Girl on the Stairs*, this TSBD office survey representative claimed that she was on the rear staircase at the same time Oswald would have been escaping from the sniper's nest but saw and heard nothing.
    A. Victoria Adams
    B. Marjorie Billings
    C. Elizabeth Wentworth
    D. Christina Mendenhall

66. Who was the Dallas motorcycle officer that questioned Oswald in the second-floor lunchroom some ninety seconds after the shooting?
    A. Roy Shaffer
    B. Marrion Baker
    C. Forrest Donofrio
    D. Chester Belmont

67. Following this encounter, Oswald left the TSBD, the only employee to do so, and boarded a bus. With traffic at a standstill, he exited the bus and hailed a taxi to his rooming house at 1026 N. Beckley Street. Who was the cab driver?
    A. Ernie Wyatt
    B. John Ritchie
    C. William Whaley
    D. Cyrus Masterson

68. En route, Oswald asked to be dropped two blocks beyond his intended stop. How much did he pay for the five- to six-minute trip?
    A. Oswald paid the fifteen-cent fare with a credit card and gave the driver no tip.
    B. Oswald gave the driver a two-dollar bill for the twenty-cent fare and a nickel tip.
    C. Oswald paid the fifty-cent fare with a five-dollar bill and gave the driver a ten-cent tip.
    D. Oswald gave the driver a dollar for the ninety-five-cent fare and told him to keep the change.

69. Shortly after returning home, Oswald left with a light-colored jacket and which handgun?
    A. Walther PP
    B. 357 Magnum
    C. 45 Colt Cobra
    D. 38 Smith & Wesson

70. As police searched the sixth floor of the TSBD, a 6.5 Mannlicher-Carcano rifle was discovered by Dallas County officers _____.
    A. Roger Craig and Justin Bushnell
    B. Luke Mooney and Harold Ferguson
    C. Joseph DeMarco and Robert Foster
    D. Seymour Weitzman and Eugene Boone

71. The weapon was initially identified as a (an) _____.
    A. M-1 Garand
    B. 7.65 Mauser
    C. Marlin 336 Carbine
    D. Mossberg 211 Repeater

72. At 1:15 p.m., Patrolman J. D. Tippit was shot by an unknown assailant at the corner of _____ in Oak Cliff section of Dallas.
    A. First and Denver Streets
    B. Sixth and Lansing Streets
    C. Tenth and Patton Streets
    D. Fifth and Crawford Streets

73. To which hospital was the gravely wounded Tippit transported?
    A. Baylor
    B. Methodist
    C. Webb Roberts
    D. Parkland Memorial

74. Of the following witnesses, who identified Oswald as the gunman?
    A. Barbara Davis
    B. Helen Markham
    C. Virginia Davis
    D. All of the above

75. Approximately fifteen minutes after and eight blocks away from the Tippit murder, Oswald was observed standing in the doorway of _____ by manager Johnny Brewer.
    A. Hardy's Shoe Store
    B. Arthur's Steak House
    C. Shaw's Drug Emporium
    D. Thomsen's Furniture Mart

76. Continuing west on Jefferson Boulevard, Oswald was next seen near the entrance to the Texas Theater. Which films were playing that day?
    A. *War Is Hell* and *Battle Cry*
    B. *Cry of Battle* and *War Is Hell*
    C. *War Wagon* and *Cry of Battle*
    D. *The War Lovers* and *Armored Assault*

77. Who was the business tycoon that briefly owned the Texas Theater in the 1930s?
    A. William Boeing
    B. Henry Swanson
    C. Walter Chrysler
    D. Howard Hughes

78. Name the cashier who alerted authorities after Oswald entered the movie house without purchasing a ticket.
    A. Julia Postal
    B. Valerie Gruber
    C. Janet Crandell
    D. Marilyn Hibbard

79. When police arrived, they entered the rear of the theater and began searching for a "suspicious-looking individual." When confronted, what was Oswald's response?[12]
    A. "I paid for my ticket!"
    B. "Well, it's all over now!"
    C. "You'll never take me alive!"
    D. "There's no reason to harass me!"

80. During a brief scuffle, one of the arresting officers was assaulted by Oswald. What was his name?
    A. Gerald Hill
    B. Mitch Wilson
    C. Nick McDonald
    D. Johnny Hunsecker

81. At police headquarters (in the Dallas Municipal Building), Oswald was taken to the office of Robbery and Homicide. Who was the legendary chief of detectives that conducted his interrogation?
    A. Captain Will Fritz
    B. Sergeant J. B. Hicks
    C. Lieutenant Bryce Ross
    D. Assistant Chief Roy Upjohn

82. When Oswald was searched, which items were found in his pockets?
    A. A bus transfer and five bullets
    B. A fingernail file and a house key
    C. A stick of gum and a switchblade
    D. A rabbit's foot and a bottle of aspirin

83. Did Oswald receive legal representation while in custody?
    A. Yes. He was defended by famed Texas attorney Joe Jamail.
    B. No. He said that he did not need a lawyer because he was innocent.
    C. Technically, yes. He said that he would defend himself if necessary.
    D. No. He wanted to be represented by New York attorney John Abt, but the two never spoke.

84. On Friday evening at 7:10 p.m. and Saturday morning at 1:30 a.m., Oswald was formally charged with which crimes?
    A. Resisting arrest and possession of a deadly weapon
    B. The murders of Patrolman J. D. Tippit and President John F. Kennedy
    C. Assaulting a police officer and making terroristic threats
    D. The murders of President John F. Kennedy and Patrolman J. D. Tippit

85. In all, how many local and federal law enforcement officials participated in or were present during Oswald's interrogations?
    A. Five
    B. Ten
    C. Fifteen
    D. Twenty-five

86. By which means did the Dallas Police record their conversations with Oswald?
   A. Dictaphone
   B. Tape recorder
   C. Stenotype machine
   D. Oswald's statements were never recorded.

87. What was Oswald's response when asked if he assassinated President Kennedy?[13]
   A. "I assassinated President Kennedy, but I did not kill Officer Tippit."
   B. "I killed Officer Tippit, but I did not assassinate President Kennedy."
   C. "I assassinated President Kennedy and I killed Officer Tippit."
   D. He never admitted to assassinating President Kennedy or to killing Officer Tippit.

88. On Saturday evening, November 24, Chief Jesse Curry informed the media that the prisoner would be moved to a more secure location the following day. To which facility was Oswald being transferred?
   A. Austin City Court
   B. Dallas County Jail
   C. Texarkana State Prison
   D. Lone Star Records Building

89. How was he to be transported?
   A. Police car
   B. Helicopter
   C. Armored van
   D. Tractor trailer

90. On Sunday morning, shortly before 11:20 a.m., Oswald was escorted from his jail cell to the basement parking garage by two Dallas detectives. Seconds later, as a WNEW-AM reporter attempted to ask him a question, local nightclub owner Jack Ruby emerged from the crowd of journalists and police and shot the alleged assassin. Who was the newsman, and what question did he ask?[14]
    A. Lou Cioffi / "Why did you do it?"
    B. Seth Kantor / "Did you shoot the president?"
    C. Bill Lawrence / "Were you part of a conspiracy?"
    D. Ike Pappas / "Do you have anything to say in your defense?"

91. Name the twenty-nine-year-old photographer with the *Dallas Times-Herald* who snapped the Pulitzer Prize–winning photograph of the shooting.
    A. Tom Mathis
    B. Carl Dempsey
    C. Robert Jackson
    D. Hugh Aynesworth

92. Who was the *Dallas Morning News* photographer that captured the second most famous photo of Ruby and Oswald, but from a different angle?
    A. Jack Beers
    B. Ross Porter
    C. Milt Jeffries
    D. Clyde Simons

93. In the ensuing chaos, which police officer tried to obtain a statement from the mortally wounded Oswald?
    A. Dickie Morris
    B. Johnny Boyer
    C. Billy Combest
    D. Robbie Wilson

94. How many minutes after being shot was Oswald pronounced dead at Parkland Hospital?
    A. 55
    B. 67
    C. 99
    D. 106

95. Following a hastily performed autopsy, Oswald's body was transported to the _____.
    A. Miller Funeral Home
    B. Affinity Memorial Center
    C. Webber-Graham Funeral Home
    D. Butler Funeral and Cremation Center

96. Which pseudonym did funeral director Paul Groody use to conceal the decedent's identity from inquisitive reporters and potential grave robbers?
    A. David Adair
    B. Jasper Raven
    C. William Bobo
    D. Robert Mintz

97. Of the following cemeteries, which was the only one that would accept Oswald's remains?
    A. Dallas Memorial Park
    B. Rose Hill Memorial Park
    C. Laurel Land Memorial Park
    D. Shady Grove Memorial Park

98. With only family members and law enforcement in attendance, who served as pallbearers at Oswald's funeral?
    A. Gravediggers
    B. Police officers
    C. Newspapermen
    D. Sanitation workers

99. A former US Army chaplain and the executive director of the Fort Worth
     Council of Churches, he was the only minister who volunteered to
     officiate at Oswald's service.
     A. James Bryant
     B. George Rudd
     C. Simon Wilson
     D. Louis Saunders

100. In what could only be described as a bizarre footnote to the Kennedy
     assassination, an eighteen-year-old named Patric Albedin purchased the
     plot next to Oswald's grave in 1975 for $175. Although no one is buried
     there, which name did he have inscribed on the headstone?
     A. NICK BEEF
     B. HAZEL NUT
     C. PETE MOSS
     D. CHUCK ROAST

CHAPTER THREE ANSWERS

1. D. New Orleans, Louisiana
2. B. heart attack
3. A. three
4. A. St. Vincent's Home
5. A. Dallas, Texas
6. B. Edwin Ekdahl
7. C. 1948
8. C. Forty-seven days
9. A. Bronx Zoo
10. A. Smith House
11. B. 118
12. C. Julius and Ethel Rosenberg
13. B. Socialism
14. C. New Orleans, Louisiana
15. D. None of the above
16. D. His mother was too controlling.
17. D. Sharpshooter
18. A. radar operator
19. C. Marine Air Control Squadron One
20. C. Russian
21. C. "Oswaldskovitch"
22. A. He claimed that his mother was ill.
23. D. He wanted to enroll at Albert Schweitzer College in Switzerland.
24. C. He allegedly saved $1,500 from his Marine Corps salary.
25. A. He slashed his wrist.
26. C. wanted to defect to Russia
27. C. 31451
28. A. Yuri Nosenko
29. D. Gorizont Electronics Factory
30. C. Priscilla Johnson and Aline Mosby

31. C. Marina Prusakova
32. B. Ministry of Internal Affairs
33. B. Pharmacy student
34. D. Less than six weeks
35. B. Ella Germann
36. D. All of the above
37. A. Richard Snyder
38. A. Spas T. Raikin
39. D. George de Morenschildt
40. B. Seaport Traders of Los Angeles, California / $29.95
41. D. None of the above
42. C. Klein's Sporting Goods of Chicago, Illinois
43. B. A. Hidell
44. B. $19.95
45. B. Marina Oswald
46. D. Imperial Reflex
47. C. Edwin Walker
48. B. Reily Coffee Company
49. B. Fair Play for Cuba Committee
50. C. Truman Capote
51. D. Carlos Bringuier
52. D. *Conversation Carte Blanche*
53. D. Mexico City, Mexico
54. D. He wanted to become a guerrilla fighter.
55. B. Valery Kostikov and Oleg Nechiporenko
56. A. Roy Truly
57. C. Earlene Roberts
58. D. Scott-Foresman
59. D. $1.25 an hour
60. D. Wedding ring and his wallet containing $170
61. B. Curtain rods
62. C. Buell Wesley Frazier
63. D. Thirty
64. A. Billy Lovelady

65. A. Victoria Adams
66. B. Marrion Baker
67. C. William Whaley
68. D. Oswald gave the driver a dollar for the ninety-five-cent fare and told him to keep the change.
69. D. .38 Smith & Wesson
70. D. Seymour Weitzman and Eugene Boone
71. B. 7.65 Mauser
72. C. Tenth and Patton Streets
73. B. Methodist
74. D. All of the above
75. A. Hardy's Shoe Store
76. B. *Cry of Battle* and *War Is Hell*
77. D. Howard Hughes
78. A. Julia Postal
79. B. "Well, it's all over now!"
80. C. Nick McDonald
81. A. Captain Will Fritz
82. A. A bus transfer and five bullets
83. D. No. He wanted to be represented by New York attorney John Abt, but the two never spoke.
84. B. The murders of Patrolman J. D. Tippit and President John F. Kennedy
85. D. Twenty-five
86. D. Oswald's statements were never recorded.
87. D. He never admitted to assassinating President Kennedy or to killing Officer Tippit.
88. B. Dallas County Jail
89. C. Armored van
90. D. Ike Pappas / "Do you have anything to say in your defense?"
91. C. Robert Jackson
92. A. Jack Beers
93. C. Billy Combest
94. D. 106
95. A. Miller Funeral Home

96. C. William Bobo
97. B. Rose Hill Memorial Park
98. C. Newspapermen
99. D. Louis Saunders
100. A. NICK BEEF

CHAPTER FOUR

JACK RUBY

1. In 1903, the parents of Jack Ruby, Joseph and Fannie Rubenstein, emigrated to the US from _____.
   A. Russia
   B. Poland
   C. Hungary
   D. Germany

2. Jacob L. Rubenstein (Ruby) was born circa March 25, 1911, in _____.
   A. Miami, Florida
   B. Chicago, Illinois
   C. Brooklyn, New York
   D. Pittsburgh, Pennsylvania

3. Ruby was the fifth of _____ children.
   A. ten
   B. eleven
   C. thirteen
   D. fourteen

4. To support his large family, the elder Rubenstein joined which union in 1904?
   A. Painters
   B. Carpenters
   C. Electricians
   D. Iron workers

5. What nickname was Rubenstein given by his coworkers?
    A. "The Kraut"
    B. "The Polack"
    C. "The Cossack"
    D. "The Bolshevik"

6. Frequently in trouble with the law, Rubenstein was often arrested for

    _____.
    A. counterfeiting
    B. armed robbery
    C. indecent exposure
    D. assault and battery

7. Incessant quarreling and physical abuse led the Rubensteins to separate in

    _____.
    A. 1919
    B. 1921
    C. 1924
    D. 1926

8. Suffering from a fractured home life, young Ruby was arrested for _____
    at the age of eleven.
    A. truancy
    B. vandalism
    C. shoplifting
    D. underage drinking

9. In 1922, Ruby was referred to which facility?
    A. Jewish Social Service Bureau
    B. Institute for Juvenile Research
    C. Webster School for Adolescents
    D. Holy Spirit Clinic for Wayward Children

10. Following a mental health evaluation, it was determined that he _____.
    A. be placed with a foster family
    B. receive electroconvulsive therapy
    C. be sent to a military boarding school
    D. receive weekly psychiatric counseling

11. After failing to graduate from high school, Ruby worked part time allegedly running errands for which notorious crime boss?
    A. Tim "Irish" Mulligan
    B. Jack "Legs" Diamond
    C. Al "Scarface" Capone
    D. Charles "Lucky" Luciano

12. It was during this period that Ruby's hair-trigger temper and aggressive nature earned him the lifelong nickname_____.
    A. "Rocky"
    B. "Sparky"
    C. "Hurricane"
    D. "Lightning"

13. At the age of twenty-two, Ruby moved to San Francisco, California, where he worked as a _____.
    A. milkman
    B. landscaper
    C. bank cashier
    D. door-to-door salesman

14. Four years later, he found employment as a _____ with the Scrap Iron and Junk Handlers Union.
    A. truck driver
    B. labor organizer
    C. union secretary
    D. machine operator

15. Between 1937 and 1938, Ruby's mother was hospitalized on two separate occasions for _____.
    A. phlebitis
    B. schizophrenia
    C. psychoneurosis
    D. obsessive compulsive behavior

16. Into which psychiatric institution was she admitted?
    A. Elgin State Hospital
    B. Telford Behavioral Health Clinic
    C. Austen Neuropsychiatric Hospital
    D. New Castle Mental Health Center

17. According to government records, Ruby's parents reconciled their marriage in _____.
    A. 1938
    B. 1939
    C. 1940
    D. 1941

18. Suffering from a heart condition exacerbated by pneumonia, Fannie Rubenstein passed away on _____.
    A. May 12, 1942
    B. June 20, 1943
    C. April 11, 1944
    D. July 25, 1945

19. Jacob Rubenstein died fourteen years later at the age of _____.
    A. eighty
    B. eighty-two
    C. eighty-four
    D. eighty-seven

20. In the early 1940s, Ruby worked for all the following businesses *except*
   _____.
   A. Mitchell Tool Company
   B. Universal Sales Company
   C. Spartan Novelty Company
   D. Globe Auto Glass Company

21. When America entered World War II, the Ruby brothers joined the armed forces. Who was the last to do so?
   A. Earl
   B. Jack
   C. Sam
   D. Hyman

22. In which branch of the military did Ruby serve?
   A. US Army
   B. US Coast Guard
   C. US Army Air Corps
   D. US Merchant Marine

23. During basic training, Ruby was required to qualify on the rifle range. Which level of proficiency did he achieve?
   A. Expert
   B. Marksman
   C. Unqualified
   D. Sharpshooter

24. Following basic training, where was Ruby stationed?
   A. Italy
   B. North Africa
   C. South Pacific
   D. United States

25. By the end of World War II, Ruby had risen to the rank of _____.
    A. lieutenant
    B. staff sergeant
    C. private first class
    D. None of the above

26. For his military service, he was awarded a _____.
    A. Bronze Star
    B. Legion of Merit
    C. Good Conduct Medal
    D. Distinguished Service Cross

27. When did Ruby receive his honorable discharge?
    A. 1944
    B. 1945
    C. 1946
    D. 1947

28. In 1947, Ruby became legally known as _____.
    A. Jack L. Ruby
    B. John L. Ruby
    C. Jack R. Ruby
    D. Jacob B. Ruby

29. That same year, Ruby moved to Dallas, Texas, to help his sister manage which club?
    A. Cotton Club Bistro
    B. Ruby's Bar and Grill
    C. Pink Peacock Lounge
    D. Singapore Supper Club

30. Ruby later changed the name of the establishment to the _____.
    A. Rodeo Lounge
    B. Silver Spur Club
    C. Harvest Moon Inn
    D. Texas Bar and Grill

31. While in "Big D," he connected with low-level underworld figures such as

    _____.
    A. Paul Weber
    B. Joseph Ficchi
    C. Edward Roland
    D. Lewis McWillie

32. Never one to shy away from the rich and famous, Ruby once surprised a
    Hollywood starlet by joining her for lunch. Who was she?
    A. Jane Russell
    B. Ava Gardner
    C. Ginger Rogers
    D. Rhonda Fleming

33. Involved in gambling at an early age, Ruby had a penchant for _____.
    A. craps
    B. roulette
    C. horse racing
    D. slot machines

34. Although Ruby avoided alcohol and tobacco, he did use appetite
    suppressants such as _____.
    A. Preludin
    B. Glarxiga
    C. Entresto
    D. Rybelsus

35. Between 1949 and 1963, how many times was Ruby arrested by the Dallas Police?
    A. two times
    B. five times
    C. eight times
    D. twelve times

36. The charges included all the following *except* _____.
    A. simple assault
    B. disturbing the peace
    C. breaking and entering
    D. carrying a concealed weapon

37. A confirmed bachelor, Ruby did however date an insurance company secretary for a period of eleven years. She would later appear as a witness at his trial.
    A. Mary Sutton
    B. Alice Nichols
    C. Connie Booth
    D. Harriet Osterman

38. In 1959, Ruby was reportedly a provisional criminal informant for which US government agency?
    A. FBI
    B. CIA
    C. DEA
    D. NSC

39. By 1963, Ruby was the owner of both the _____.
    A. Carousel Club and Lion's Den
    B. Vegas Club and Carousel Club
    C. Carousel Club and Odessa Lounge
    D. Blue Point Bar & Grill and Carousel Club

40. When asked to describe the Carousel Club, Ruby said it is a _____ [15]
    A. "f***ing classy joint."
    B. "way to pay the rent."
    C. "bar for cops and crooks."
    D. "place to relax and have a good time."

41. On the day of the assassination, where was Ruby?
    A. Playing cards with his neighbor
    B. Visiting one of his sick employees
    C. Shopping at the Rexall Drug Store
    D. In the advertising office of the *Dallas Morning News*

42. Which was Ruby's reaction when he learned of President Kennedy's death?
    A. He fainted.
    B. He had no reaction.
    C. He became visibly upset.
    D. He laughed uncontrollably.

43. How many times did Ruby "stalk" Oswald at Dallas Police headquarters?
    A. One
    B. Two
    C. Three
    D. None of the above

44. On the evening of November 22, Ruby attended a news conference posing as which of the following?
    A. Janitor
    B. Reporter
    C. Deliveryman
    D. Police officer

45. When District Attorney Henry Wade incorrectly identified Oswald as a member of the Free Cuba Committee, what did Ruby shout from the back of the room?[16]
    A. "Henry, that's the Fair Play for Cuba Committee."
    B. "Nope, you mean the Committee for Cuban Fair Play."
    C. "With all due respect, Oswald was with the Committee for Cuban Affairs."
    D. "Excuse me Mr. Wade, I think you mean the Fair Play Committee for Cubans."

46. On the morning of November 24, Ruby drove to the downtown Western Union office. Which type of car was he driving?
    A. 1956 Ford
    B. 1957 Cadillac
    C. 1959 Rambler
    D. 1960 Oldsmobile

47. In the front seat of the vehicle was his most prized possession. What was it?
    A. His dachshund
    B. His hunting rifle
    C. His 18K gold watch
    D. His mother's wedding ring

48. To whom did Ruby make a wire transfer?
    A. Hyman Ruby, his older brother
    B. Joe Campisi, a business associate
    C. Horace Levine, a childhood friend
    D. Karen Bennett, a stripper at the Carousel Club

49. How much money did he send?
    A. $25
    B. $50
    C. $125
    D. $200

50. After leaving the Western Union office, Ruby walked a short distance to the city jail where Oswald was being held. Who was the police officer that allowed Ruby to gain access to the building via the entrance ramp?
   A. Vance Elroy
   B. Roy Vaughn
   C. Ted Williams
   D. Melvyn Thomas

51. Which type of handgun was Ruby carrying in his suit coat pocket?
   A. .44 Magnum
   B. .38 Colt Cobra
   C. .256 Winchester
   D. .38 Smith & Wesson

52. How long did Ruby wait in the basement garage before Oswald appeared?
   A. Three minutes
   B. Seven minutes
   C. Twelve minutes
   D. Fifteen minutes

53. At 11:21 a.m., as the man accused of killing President Kennedy and Officer Tippit came into view, Ruby raised his gun, lunged forward, and fired one shot into his abdomen. Which finger did Ruby use to pull the trigger?
   A. The index finger of his left hand
   B. The ring finger of his right hand
   C. The pinky finger of his left hand
   D. The middle finger of his right hand

54. In the chaos that followed, who was the TV correspondent that yelled "He's been shot. He's been shot. Lee Oswald has been shot!"?[17]
   A. Tom Pettit
   B. Frank McGee
   C. Douglas Edwards
   D. Howard K. Smith

55. As Ruby was wrestled to the ground by police, which of the following did he shout?[18]
    A. "Wait, I did you guys a favor!"
    B. "You all know me. I'm Jack Ruby!"
    C. "Why not? The dirty little rat had it coming!"
    D. "I'm Jack Ruby. I did this for Jackie and the kids!"

56. Who was the detective that pried the gun from Ruby's hand? In 2015, he was posthumously awarded the Dallas Police Department's Medal of Valor for his bravery that day.
    A. L. C. Graves
    B. Darryl Cummings
    C. R. C. Montgomery
    D. Eugene Cosworth

57. How many reporters and police officers were present when Ruby shot Oswald?
    A. 52
    B. 65
    C. 87
    D. 125

58. Which was the only TV network to provide live coverage of the shooting?
    A. ABC
    B. CBS
    C. NBC
    D. PBS

59. Taken into custody, Ruby was "booked" or "processed." The procedure included the confiscation of his personal property, and he was fingerprinted and photographed. What was Ruby's mugshot number?
    A. 34902
    B. 36398
    C. 37411
    D. 38645

60. When asked why he shot Oswald, how did Ruby respond?
    A. He was pressured to do so to conceal a Mafia plot.
    B. He needed to avenge the death of his favorite president.
    C. He shot Oswald by mistake. He was trying to kill Dallas Police Chief Jesse Curry.
    D. He wanted to spare Mrs. Kennedy the anguish of returning to Dallas for a trial.

61. At first, whom did Ruby want as his defense lawyer?
    A. F. Lee Bailey
    B. Tom Howard
    C. George Baker
    D. Percy Foreman

62. Ultimately, the flamboyant Melvin Belli was installed as lead counsel. Who made the decision to hire Belli?
    A. Ruby's sister Eva
    B. Ruby's brother Earl
    C. Ruby's nephew David
    D. Ruby's brother Sidney

63. Known as "The King of Torts," Belli had represented such celebrated clients as _____.
    A. Mae West and Errol Flynn
    B. John Wayne and Shirley Temple
    C. Mickey Rooney and Judy Garland
    D. Robert Mitchum and Marilyn Monroe

64. How much did Belli receive for his legal services, and who paid the bill?
    A. $150,000 / The Ruby family
    B. $200,000 / The *Dallas Morning News*
    C. $350,000 / Texas industrialist H. L. Hunt
    D. He represented Ruby *pro bono*.

65. On December 23, 1963, the first of Ruby's _____ bail hearings were held.
    A. two
    B. five
    C. seven
    D. eleven

66. Entering a plea of not guilty by reason of insanity, Belli's defense strategy
    was based on the premise that Ruby suffered from which of the following
    brain disorders?
    A. Dementia
    B. Schizophrenia
    C. Myopic Cancer
    D. Psychomotor epilepsy

67. Convinced that Ruby would not receive a fair trial in Dallas, Belli
    unsuccessfully argued for a change of venue. At the hearing, which
    prominent department store executive testified for the defense?
    A. Andrew Saks of Saks Fifth Avenue
    B. Stanley Marcus of Neiman Marcus
    C. Edwin Goodman of Bergdorf Goodman
    D. Joseph Bloomingdale of Bloomingdale's

68. Of the nine hundred people who were summoned for jury duty, how many
    were interviewed?
    A. 168
    B. 234
    C. 347
    D. 498

69. How long did the selection process last?
    A. Twelve days
    B. Fourteen days
    C. Eighteen days
    D. Nineteen days

70. When it was chosen, what was the composition of the jury?
    A. Ten men and two women
    B. Eight men and four women
    C. Five men and seven women
    D. Seven men and five women

71. How many alternate jurors were selected?
    A. One
    B. Two
    C. Four
    D. None

72. While awaiting trial, Ruby was interviewed for a syndicated newspaper story. What was the feature entitled?
    A. "Dallas Executioner"
    B. "The Story of My Life"
    C. "Jack Ruby: In My Own Words"
    D. "Why I Shot Kennedy's Assassin"

73. According to the article, what was Ruby thinking just before he shot Oswald?[19]
    A. "He acted like a punk. The little rat deserved to die for what he did."
    B. "He looked like a killer. I couldn't believe he murdered President Kennedy."
    C. "He appeared to be guilty. The smirk on his face made me want to throw up."
    D. "He looked like a creep. But he didn't look like he could have killed our president all alone."

74. In *Kennedy's Avenger: Assassination, Conspiracy, and the Forgotten Trial of Jack Ruby*, authors Dan Abrams and David Fisher claimed that Ruby was paid for the story. How much did he receive?
    A. $19,000
    B. $24,000
    C. $28,000
    D. $32,000

75. Ruby was also interviewed by the celebrated columnist and panelist on the CBS game show, *What's My Line?* Who was she?
    A. Ann Landers
    B. Hedda Hopper
    C. Louella Parsons
    D. Dorothy Kilgallen

76. On which date did the trial begin?
    A. March 4, 1964
    B. March 9, 1964
    C. March 11, 1964
    D. March 20, 1964

77. Which of the following was the case title?
    A. *Jack Ruby v. The United States*
    B. *The State of Texas v. Jacob Ruby*
    C. *Jacob Rubenstein v. The United States*
    D. *The State of Texas v. Jack Rubenstein*

78. The proceedings were held in the Criminal Courts Building, an eleven-story facility in downtown Dallas. Opened in 1915, it included a chapel, an infirmary, an execution room, and a jail, which had earlier housed Depression-era gangster _____.
    A. Doc Barker
    B. Alvin Karpas
    C. John Dillinger
    D. Clyde Barrow

79. Approximately how many local, national, and international journalists covered the trial?
    A. One hundred
    B. Two hundred
    C. Four hundred
    D. Seven hundred

80. Which attorney(s) served on Ruby's defense team?
    A. Elmer Gertz
    B. Phil Burleson
    C. Simon Porter
    D. A and B

81. All the following prosecuted the case *except* _____.
    A. Frank Watts
    B. Henry Wade
    C. Marshall Evans
    D. William Alexander

82. Who was the presiding judge?
    A. Winston Lynch
    B. Logan Schmidt
    C. Myron Pettigrew
    D. Joe B. Brown Sr.

83. Of the sixty-four people who testified, how many were physicians?
    A. Eight
    B. Twelve
    C. Fourteen
    D. Seventeen

84. How many Dallas Police officers provided testimony?
    A. Nine
    B. Eleven
    C. Twelve
    D. Eighteen

85. Who was the decorated World War II veteran and welterweight boxing champion that served as a Ruby character witness?
    A. Fritzie Zivic
    B. Jack Britton
    C. Barney Ross
    D. Rocky Graziano

86. During the trial many unsubstantiated claims were leaked to the media. They included all the following *except* _____.
    A. Ruby had sold guns to Fidel Castro
    B. Ruby was the second gunman in Dealey Plaza
    C. Ruby had been seen in the Carousel Club with Oswald
    D. Ruby and Governor Connally had conspired to assassinate JFK

87. How many lawyers took part in closing arguments?
    A. Two
    B. Four
    C. Seven
    D. Eleven

88. After ten days of testimony and cross-examination, the jurors received their instructions from the bench on _____.
    A. March 14, 1964
    B. March 19, 1964
    C. March 21. 1964
    D. March 30, 1964

89. How long did they deliberate?
    A. Two hours and nineteen minutes
    B. Four hours and thirty-six minutes
    C. Seven hours and fifty-eight minutes
    D. Eleven hours and twenty-six minutes

90. Which verdict did the jury render?
    A. Guilty of manslaughter (death penalty)
    B. Guilty by reason of insanity (life in prison)
    C. Guilty of murder with malice (death penalty)
    D. Guilty of murder with special circumstances (twenty years in prison)

91. Although convicted in the death of Oswald, rumors of Ruby's involvement in an assassination plot persisted. Who petitioned to have Ruby testify before the Warren Commission (WC)?
    A. His brother, Sam Ruby
    B. His lawyer, Melvin Belli
    C. His friend, George Senator
    D. His sister, Eileen Kaminsky

92. Name two of the WC members who questioned Ruby on June 7, 1964.
    A. Hale Boggs and Earl Warren
    B. Earl Warren and Gerald Ford
    C. John J. McCloy and Earl Warren
    D. Earl Warren and Richard Russell

93. Following their meeting, Warren concluded that _____.
    A. Ruby was a contract killer for the Mafia
    B. Ruby knew Oswald before November 22, 1963
    C. Ruby should receive a medal for shooting Oswald
    D. Ruby had not known or seen Oswald before the assassination

94. In October of 1966, which three-judge panel overturned Ruby's conviction?
    A. US Circuit Court of Appeals
    B. Texas Court of Criminal Appeals
    C. Dallas County Common Pleas Court
    D. Texas Court of Appeals for the Eastern District

95. On what grounds did the court make its decision?
    A. There was evidence of jury tampering.
    B. One of the prosecuting attorneys was anti-Semitic.
    C. Four of the prosecution witnesses had been bribed.
    D. Ruby's initial statements to police were inadmissible.

96. In which city and state was the new trial scheduled to take place?
    A. Galveston, Texas
    B. Zachary, Louisiana
    C. Wichita Falls, Texas
    D. Manhattan, Kansas

97. Diagnosed with inoperable cancer in December of 1966, Ruby did not live
    to have his "second" day in court. He died on _____.
    A. January 3, 1967
    B. January 5, 1967
    C. January 7, 1967
    D. January 9, 1967

98. Which lawyer would later capitalize on the Ruby trial by authoring a book
    entitled *Dallas Justice*, and appearing on the TV series *Star Trek*?
    A. Melvin Belli
    B. Elmer Gertz
    C. F. Lee Bailey
    D. William Kunstler

99. In what was thought to be the closing chapter in the JFK assassination
    investigation, the House Select Committee on Assassinations (HSCA)
    concluded in 1979 that _____.
    A. Ruby *may* have been part of a conspiracy
    B. Ruby was the second gunman in Dealey Plaza
    C. Ruby killed Oswald to avenge the assassination of JFK
    D. Ruby was acting as a hitman for the Mafia when he shot Oswald

100. Ironically, it was Jack Ruby who would have the last word. On December 26, 1991, the handgun he used to kill Oswald was sold at auction to Florida real estate developer Anthony Pugliese. How much was paid for the infamous piece of history?

A. $125,000

B. $220,000

C. $345,000

D. $400,000

Chapter Four Answers

1.   B. Poland
2.   B. Chicago, Illinois
3.   A. ten
4.   B. Carpenters
5.   C. "The Cossack"
6.   D. assault and battery
7.   B. 1921
8.   A. truancy
9.   B. Institute for Juvenile Research
10.   A. be placed with a foster family
11.   C. Al "Scarface" Capone
12.   B. "Sparky"
13.   D. door-to-door salesman
14.   B. labor organizer
15.   C. psychoneurosis
16.   A. Elgin State Hospital
17.   C. 1940
18.   C. April 11, 1944
19.   D. eighty-seven
20.   A. Mitchell Tool Company
21.   B. Jack
22.   C. US Army Air Corps
23.   D. Sharpshooter
24.   D. United States
25.   C. private first class
26.   C. Good Conduct Medal
27.   C. 1946
28.   A. Jack L. Ruby
29.   D. Singapore Supper Club
30.   B. Silver Spur Club

31. D. Lewis McWillie
32. D. Rhonda Fleming
33. C. horse racing
34. A. Preludin
35. C. eight times
36. C. breaking and entering
37. B. Alice Nichols
38. A. FBI
39. B. Vegas Club and Carousel Club
40. A. "f***ing classy joint."
41. D. In the advertising office of the *Dallas Morning News*
42. C. He became visibly upset.
43. C. Three
44. B. Reporter
45. A. "Henry, that's the Fair Play for Cuba Committee."
46. D. 1960 Oldsmobile
47. A. His dachshund
48. D. Karen Bennett, a stripper at the Carousel Club
49. A. $25
50. B. Roy Vaughn
51. B. .38 Colt Cobra
52. A. Three minutes
53. D. The middle finger of his right hand.
54. A. Tom Pettit
55. B. "You all know me. I'm Jack Ruby!"
56. A. L. C. Graves
57. D. 125
58. C. NBC
59. B. 36398
60. D. He wanted to spare Mrs. Kennedy the anguish of returning to Dallas for a trial.
61. B. Tom Howard
62. B. Ruby's brother Earl

63. A. Mae West and Errol Flynn
64. D. He represented Ruby *pro bono*.
65. A. two
66. D. Psychomotor epilepsy
67. B. Stanley Marcus of Neiman Marcus
68. A. 168
69. B. Fourteen days
70. B. Eight men and four women
71. D. None
72. B. "The Story of My Life"
73. D. "He looked like a creep. But he didn't look like he could have killed our president alone."
74. C. $28,000
75. D. Dorothy Kilgallen
76. A. March 4, 1964
77. D. *The State of Texas v. Jack Rubenstein*
78. D. Clyde Barrow
79. C. Four hundred
80. D. A and B
81. C. Marshall Evans
82. D. Joe B. Brown Sr.
83. D. Seventeen
84. C. Twelve
85. C. Barney Ross
86. D. Ruby and Governor Connally had conspired to assassinate JFK
87. C. Seven
88. A. March 14, 1964
89. A. Two hours and nineteen minutes
90. C. Guilty of murder with malice (death penalty)
91. D. His sister, Eileen Kaminsky
92. B. Earl Warren and Gerald Ford
93. D. Ruby had not known or seen Oswald before the assassination
94. B. Texas Court of Criminal Appeals
95. D. Ruby's initial statements to police were inadmissible

96.   C. Wichita Falls, Texas
97.   A. January 3, 1967
98.   A. Melvin Belli
99.   A. Ruby *may* have been part of a conspiracy
100. B. $220,000

Chapter Five

The Warren Commission

1. To investigate the circumstances surrounding the assassination of President John F. Kennedy and to quell all rumors of a conspiracy, a "blue-ribbon" panel was appointed by President Lyndon Johnson on _____.
   A. November 23, 1963
   B. November 28, 1963
   C. November 29, 1963
   D. November 30, 1963

2. Unofficially known as the Warren Commission, it was officially titled the _____.
   A. Executive Committee on the Death of John F. Kennedy
   B. US Government Inquiry into the Murder of President John F. Kennedy
   C. President's Commission on the Assassination of President John F. Kennedy
   D. Federal Inquiry into the Deaths of President Kennedy and Lee Harvey Oswald

3. Which federal law created the panel?
   A. House Resolution 1594
   B. Executive Order 11130
   C. Senate Resolution 1271
   D. Presidential Order 1963

4. Although Chief Justice Earl Warren was "persuaded" to lead the investigation, who was President Johnson's first choice?
   A. Allen Dulles
   B. Dean Acheson
   C. J. Edgar Hoover
   D. George Marshall

5. To serve as chief counsel, Warren named J. Lee Rankin, a former US solicitor general in the _____ administration.
   A. Hoover
   B. Truman
   C. Roosevelt
   D. Eisenhower

6. Which fellow Californian did Warren prefer for the position?
   A. Harold Sanders
   B. Warren Olney III
   C. Jerry Buchmeyer Jr.
   D. Nicholas Katzenbach

7. One of fourteen assistant or junior counsels, he was appointed Rankin's special assistant.
   A. Philip Barson
   B. Lloyd Weinreb
   C. Charles Shaffer
   D. Norman Redlich

8. The WC held its first meeting on _____.
   A. December 5, 1963
   B. December 10, 1963
   C. December 23, 1963
   D. December 31, 1963

9. Where in Washington, DC, was the commission's headquarters located?
   A. Supreme Court
   B. US Post Office Building
   C. National Portrait Gallery
   D. Veterans of Foreign Wars Building

10. Excluding Warren, the commission was comprised of _____ current or former public servants.
    A. six
    B. four
    C. twelve
    D. fourteen

11. Who were the two US senators that served on the commission?
    A. Wilbur Mills and Richard Russell
    B. Thomas Dodd and Warren Magnuson
    C. John Sherman Cooper and Allen Ellender
    D. Richard Russell and John Sherman Cooper

12. Name the only two nonelected members on the panel.
    A. Gerald Ford and Allen Dulles
    B. Hale Boggs and Richard Russell
    C. Allen Dulles and John J. McCloy
    D. John Sherman Cooper and Hale Boggs

13. Which commission member initially refused to join the investigation because he disagreed with Warren's liberal views.
    A. Hale Boggs
    B. Gerald Ford
    C. Richard Russell
    D. John J. McCloy

14. A former director of the CIA, he withheld critical information from the WC regarding the attempted assassination of Fidel Castro.
    A. Porter Goss
    B. Allen Dulles
    C. John J. McCloy
    D. William Donovan

15. Because of this commissioner's demanding legislative schedule, he was present for only six percent of the witness testimony.
    A. Hale Boggs
    B. Gerald Ford
    C. Richard Russell
    D. John Sherman Cooper

16. The quote, "Truth is our only goal" is attributed to which member of the WC?[20]
    A. Earl Warren
    B. Gerald Ford
    C. John J. McCloy
    D. Richard Russell

17. Which crucial evidence was never examined by the commission?
    A. Oswald's rifle
    B. JFK's limousine
    C. Ruby's telephone records
    D. JFK's autopsy photographs and X-rays

18. This WC member would later disappear on a campaign flight to Juneau, Alaska, in 1972.
    A. Hale Boggs
    B. Nick Begich
    C. Allen Dulles
    D. Robert Giaimo

19. A Republican congressman from Michigan, he was the FBI's informant on the commission.
    A. Philip Hart
    B. Hale Boggs
    C. Gerald Ford
    D. Patrick Miles

20. Before serving on the WC, this Washington insider had been assistant secretary of war and adviser to four presidents.
    A. John J. McCloy
    B. Milton Hershey
    C. Richard Russell
    D. John Sherman Cooper

21. In 1933, while serving with the US delegation at the League of Nations, this future commissioner met Adolf Hitler.
    A. Hale Boggs
    B. Allen Dulles
    C. Gerald Ford
    D. J. Lee Rankin

22. Leslie Lynch King Jr. was the birth name of which WC member?
    A. Hale Boggs
    B. Earl Warren
    C. Gerald Ford
    D. Allen Dulles

23. In a strange twist of fate, this commissioner was the target of two assassination attempts in 1975.
    A. Gerald Ford
    B. John J. McCloy
    C. Richard Russell
    D. John Sherman Cooper

24. Who was the oldest member on the WC?
    A. Earl Warren
    B. Gerald Ford
    C. J. Lee Rankin
    D. Richard Russell

25. In 1974, this commissioner became the first US ambassador to East Germany.
    A. J. Lee Rankin
    B. John J. McCloy
    C. Richard Russell
    D. John Sherman Cooper

26. Which of the following WC members did *not* express reservations with the final report?
    A. Hale Boggs
    B. Earl Warren
    C. Richard Russell
    D. John Sherman Cooper

27. This commissioner did *not* testify before the HSCA.
    A. Earl Warren
    B. J. Lee Rankin
    C. John J. McCloy
    D. John Sherman Cooper

28. Name the two members of the WC who are buried in Arlington National Cemetery.
    A. Allen Dulles and Hale Boggs
    B. Richard Russell and John J. McCloy
    C. Gerald Ford and John Sherman Cooper
    D. John Sherman Cooper and Earl Warren

29. Who was the last surviving member of the Commission?
    A. Gerald Ford
    B. Earl Warren
    C. Richard Russell
    D. John J. McCloy

30. Before the WC began its probe, there was an implicit understanding that most of the work would be conducted by the _____.
    A. FBI
    B. WC counsels
    C. US Secret Service
    D. Department of Justice

31. Which Commission lawyer was responsible for probing Oswald's background?
    A. Joseph Ball
    B. Leon Hubert
    C. Richard Mosk
    D. David Slawson

32. Of the following, who was charged with researching Jack Ruby?
    A. Burt Griffin
    B. David Belin
    C. Samuel Stern
    D. Melvin Eisenberg

33. Who was responsible for investigating conspiracy theories, foreign and domestic?
    A. Burt Griffin
    B. Albert Jenner
    C. David Slawson
    D. Francis Adams

34. This assistant counsel served as liaison between the commission and the Department of Justice.
    A. Martin Miller
    B. Francis Adams
    C. Victor Sheehan
    D. Howard Willens

35. Who is recognized as the author of the highly controversial "single-bullet theory"?
    A. Leon Hubert
    B. Arlen Specter
    C. Wesley Liebeler
    D. Howard Willens

36. Name the assistant counsel who later became a US senator from Pennsylvania.
    A. Joseph Ball
    B. Arlen Specter
    C. Melvin Eisenberg
    D. William Coleman Jr.

37. According to *New York Times* investigative journalist Philp Shenon, a commission lawyer secretly interviewed Fidel Castro regarding the assassination. Who was he?
    A. David Belin
    B. Albert Jenner
    C. Norman Redlich
    D. William Coleman Jr.

38. Which of the following junior counsels later authored books about the assassination?
    A. Leon Hubert and Joseph Ball
    B. Davide Belin and Howard Willens
    C. Melvin Eisenberg and Samuel Stern
    D. Norman Redlich and Wesley Liebeler

39. A Harvard-trained lawyer who was named Secretary of Transportation in 1975, he was the only African American to serve on the legal staff of the WC.
    A. John Ely
    B. Arthur Marmor
    C. Edward Conroy
    D. William Coleman Jr.

40. Of the twelve commission staffers, who was the youngest?
    A. John Hart Ely
    B. Edward Conroy
    C. Alfred Goldberg
    D. Murray Laulicht

41. A practicing attorney, who later became a legal assistant with the Georgia Court of Appeals, she was the only female on the WC staff.
    A. Irene Laufler
    B. Margaret Tobias
    C. Alfredda Scobey
    D. Constance Revilla

42. Of the thirty-four commission members, lawyers, and staffers, how many graduated from Ivy League schools?
    A. Eleven
    B. Twelve
    C. Sixteen
    D. Eighteen

43. Which public law gave the WC authority to subpoena witnesses and obtain evidentiary material?
    A. 55-703
    B. 72-890
    C. 88-202
    D. 96-101

44. How many witnesses testified before and gave sworn affidavits to the commission?
    A. 325
    B. 486
    C. 550
    D. 667

45. Who was the first witness deposed?
    A. John Connally
    B. Marina Oswald
    C. Nellie Connally
    D. Marguerite Oswald

46. Name the US Marine Corps weapons expert who testified that Oswald possessed the skills necessary to assassinate President Kennedy.
    A. Richard Call
    B. James Zahm
    C. Peter Connor
    D. Nelson Delgado

47. Which of these Dealey Plaza witnesses was never questioned by the commission?
    A. Amos Euins
    B. Danny Arce
    C. Avery Davis
    D. Emmett Hudson

48. A passenger in Vice President Johnson's car, he was the only US senator to appear before the WC.
    A. John Tower
    B. Lloyd Bentsen
    C. William Blakely
    D. Ralph Yarborough

49. Which witness made the dubious claim that she saw Jack Ruby at the scene of the assassination when he was supposedly elsewhere?
    A. Jean Hill
    B. Mary Miller
    C. Linda Willis
    D. Marie Muchmore

50. This New York attorney and future critic of the WC testified that the incriminating backyard photographs of Oswald were forgeries.
    A. Mark Lane
    B. Allen Melvin
    C. Mitchell Welker
    D. Harold Rothman

51. Who were the only two witnesses to provide the commission with written statements?
    A. Marina and Robert Oswald
    B. Lyndon and Lady Bird Johnson
    C. Robert McNamara and Robert Kennedy
    D. J. Edgar Hoover and Nicholas Katzenbach

52. A Cuban refugee and anti-Castro sympathizer, she testified that in September 1963, she was visited by three men, one of whom was named Leon Oswald.
    A. Sylvia Odio
    B. Camila Gomez
    C. Valeria Machado
    D. Guadalupe Quesada

53. How many Parkland Hospital doctors appeared before the WC?
    A. Eleven
    B. Thirteen
    C. Fourteen
    D. Seventeen

54. Name the car salesman who testified that weeks before the assassination, Oswald test-drove a Mercury Comet at a high rate of speed.
    A. Prentiss Smith
    B. Albert Bogard
    C. Mark McDonald
    D. Travis Schwimmer

55. According to this WC witness, JFK's last words were, "My God, I'm hit!"[21]
    A. Frank Yeager
    B. Roy Kellerman
    C. Nellie Connally
    D. Lubert DeFreese

56. Which Kennedy cabinet officials gave testimony before the commission?
    A. Douglas Dillon and Dean Rusk
    B. William Wurtz and Stewart Udall
    C. Abraham Ribicoff and Luther Hodges
    D. Robert McNamara and Orville Freeman

57. A clinical psychologist, he testified that as a youth, Oswald suffered from a "personality pattern disturbance" brought on by a "lack of affection, absence of life, and rejection by a self-involved and conflicted."[22]
    A. Peter Baumann
    B. Renatus Hartogs
    C. Donald Cameron
    D. Stephen Bergman

58. Name the witness who referred to the assassination weapon as "the fateful rifle of Lee Oswald."[23]
    A. Marina Oswald
    B. Nellie Connally
    C. Ladybird Johnson
    D. Jacqueline Kennedy

59. Of the following members of JFK's motorcycle escort, which one did *not* testify before the commission?
    A. Bobby Hargis
    B. Glen McBride
    C. Billy Joe Martin
    D. Clyde Haygood

60. This witness asserted his Fifth Amendment right to self-incrimination multiple times during questioning.
    A. Oliver Morris
    B. Robert Surrey
    C. Gilbert Krause
    D. Clifford Mercer

61. Which TSBD employee told WC lawyers that when the shooting began, he could hear the "bolt action of the rifle"?[24]
    A. John Gedney
    B. Thomas Bowe
    C. Harold Norman
    D. Gerald Earlington

62. A World War II veteran who appeared before the commission, he held the distinction of having witnessed both the Japanese attack on Pearl Harbor and the JFK assassination.
    A. Phillip Willis
    B. Robert Altieri
    C. Andrew Murray
    D. Thomas Winston

63. Which future US Speaker of the House was a passenger in the Dallas motorcade, but did *not* testify before the commission?
    A. Carl Albert
    B. Jim Wright
    C. Thomas Foley
    D. Newt Gingrich

64. This Parkland Hospital employee was questioned by the WC about his discovery of the so-called "magic bullet."
A. Cecil Andrews
B. Darrell Tomlinson
C. Jeremiah Holstein
D. Walter Donaldson

65. Which Dallas Police officer told commissioners that he could not positively identify Oswald's prints on the rifle?
A. J. C. Day
B. R. J. Hansell
C. G. D. Dougherty
D. R. L. Studebaker

66. Name the witness who allegedly saw Oswald in the sixth-floor window of the TSBD at the time of the assassination.
A. Roy Truly
B. George Ewell
C. William Shelley
D. Howard Brennan

67. Of the following Secret Service agents, which one did *not* testify before the WC?
A. Clint Hill
B. John Ready
C. William Greer
D. Roy Kellerman

68. A CBS reporter, he was the only network journalist called before the commission.
A. Nelson Benton
B. Charles Osgood
C. Douglas Edwards
D. Robert Pierpoint

69. Who was the WC witness that answered more than five thousand questions?
    A. Ruth Paine
    B. Lillian Murret
    C. Jeanne Dupree
    D. Earlene Roberts

70. This signal supervisor for the Union Terminal Railroad told commissioners that after the final shot he observed a puff of smoke in the area of the grassy knoll.
    A. Lee Bowers
    B. James Tague
    C. Ken Marsden
    D. S. M. Holland

71. All of the following were called before the WC and the HSCA *except*
    _____.
    A. Earl Ruby
    B. Peter Gregory
    C. Richard Helms
    D. Thomas Kelley

72. How many witnesses to the Tippit shooting were questioned by the commission?
    A. Six
    B. Ten
    C. Eleven
    D. Thirteen

73. Which Oswald acquaintance and WC witness committed suicide before he could meet with HSCA investigators?
    A. Thomas Ray
    B. Lev Aronsen
    C. Teofil Meller
    D. George de Mohrenschildt

74. Of the following Dallas Police officers, which one appeared before the HSCA, but not the WC?
A. H. B. McLain
B. J. F. Timoney
C. K. A. Crawford
D. R. W. Simmons

75. Name the physician who was questioned about his psychiatric evaluation of Jack Ruby.
A. George Bell
B. Aaron Davis
C. William Beavers
D. Broderick Everson

76. Which was the last witness deposed by the commission?
A. Jesse Curry
B. Glen Bennett
C. John Gallagher
D. Woodrow Wiggins

77. How many WC witnesses died within two years of the assassination?
A. Eight
B. Twelve
C. Fifteen
D. Twenty-six

78. On September 24, 1964, the WC submitted its findings to President Johnson. How many pages did the Warren Report contain?
A. 643
B. 769
C. 888
D. 945

79. After a nine-month investigation, the commission concluded all the following *except* _____.
A. President John F. Kennedy was assassinated by Lee Harvey Oswald
B. Oswald fired three shots from an Austrian-made rifle on the sixth floor of the TSBD
C. Jack Ruby, acting on his own initiative, shot and killed Lee Harvey Oswald
D. the commission found *no credible* evidence of a foreign or domestic conspiracy

80. Which major recommendation was made by the WC?
A. Presidential motorcades should be prohibited.
B. Campaigning in the South should be discouraged.
C. Future presidents should wear a bulletproof vest.
D. Secret Service protection methods should be reevaluated.

81. On November 23, 1964, the complete report including the testimonies and evidence was released. In total, how many volumes were published?
A. Twenty-one
B. Twenty-two
C. Twenty-five
D. Twenty-six

82. How many exhibits were included in the report?
A. 3154
B. 3357
C. 3592
D. 3623

83. In which volume of the report will you find the testimony of the Bethesda autopsists?
A. II
B. IV
C. VII
D. XII

84. Which WC exhibit is Oswald's 6.5 Mannlicher-Carcano rifle?
    A. No. 107
    B. No. 129
    C. No. 139
    D. No. 140

85. In which volumes will you find the testimony of FBI firearms expert Cortlandt Cunningham?
    A. I, III, IV
    B. II, III, VII
    C. VII, VII, X
    D. IX, XI, XIII

86. This commission exhibit is a photograph taken at Lee Harvey Oswald's funeral.
    A. No. 165
    B. No. 181
    C. No. 199
    D. No. 204

87. Where in the report will you find the testimony of Jack Ruby?
    A. Volumes I and XII
    B. Volumes II and VII
    C. Volumes V and XIV
    D. Volumes VII and VII

88. This commission exhibit is a postcard from Lee Harvey Oswald to Robert Oswald.
    A. No. 200
    B. No. 250
    C. No. 324
    D. No. 343

89. In this volume you will find the testimony of J. Edgar Hoover.
    A. II
    B. III
    C. IV
    D. None of the above

90. Which WC exhibit is a letter from Lee Harvey Oswald to his mother?
    A. No.153
    B. No. 160
    C. No. 186
    D. No. 197

91. How many volumes contain the testimony of Attorney General Robert Kennedy?
    A. Two
    B. Four
    C. Eight
    D. He never testified

92. Which WC exhibits are photographs of JFK's limousine?
    A. Nos. 278 to 282
    B. Nos. 344 to 346
    C. Nos. 678 to 702
    D. Nos. 802 to 805

93. In Volume XII is the testimony of the three Dallas policemen who apprehended Jack Ruby. Which one was not an arresting officer?
    A. B. H. Combest
    B. Patrick Dean
    C. Don Ray Archer
    D. Bernard Clardy

94. These commission exhibits are the wrist X-rays of Governor John Connally.
    A. Nos. 690 to 693
    B. Nos. 701 to 704
    C. Nos. 811 to 815
    D. Nos. 902 to 906

95. Although President Johnson publicly accepted the findings of the WC, he privately suspected that (the) _____ was responsible for JFK's death.
    A. CIA
    B. Mafia
    C. Fidel Castro
    D. Soviet Union

96. In its critique of the Warren Report, this Pulitzer Prize–winning newspaper stated that "it should destroy the basis for conspiracy theories that have grown weed-like in this country."[25]
    A. *The New York Times*
    B. *The Philadelphia Inquirer*
    C. *The Christian Science Monitor*
    D. *The Atlanta Journal Constitution*

97. Which magazine, in its October 16, 1964, issue, referred to the Warren Report as the "most conscientious documentation of facts ever assembled."[26]
    A. *Time*
    B. *Newsweek*
    C. *Life Magazine*
    D. *National Review*

98. Following the release of the commission's findings, _____ of Americans believed that Oswald was the lone assassin.
    A. 51 percent
    B. 64 percent
    C. 76 percent
    D. 87 percent

99. By 2013, _____ of Americans believed that JFK's death was the result of a conspiracy.
    A. 52 percent
    B. 61 percent
    C. 82 percent
    D. 94 percent

100. Which federal agency became the depository for all WC materials?
     A. National Archives
     B. Smithsonian Institute
     C. Bureau of Presidential History
     D. Council For Historic Preservation

CHAPTER FIVE ANSWERS

1. C. November 29, 1963
2. C. President's Commission on the Assassination of President John F. Kennedy
3. B. Executive Order 11130
4. A. Allen Dulles
5. D. Eisenhower
6. B. Warren Olney III
7. D. Norman Redlich
8. A. December 5, 1963
9. D. Veterans of Foreign Wars Building
10. A. six
11. D. Richard Russell and John Sherman Cooper
12. C. Allen Dulles and John J. McCloy
13. C. Richard Russell
14. B. Allen Dulles
15. C. Richard Russell
16. A. Earl Warren
17. D. JFK's autopsy photographs and X-rays
18. A. Hale Boggs
19. C. Gerald Ford
20. A. John J. McCloy
21. B. Allen Dulles
22. C. Gerald Ford
23. A. Gerald Ford
24. A. Earl Warren
25. D. John Sherman Cooper
26. B. Earl Warren
27. A. Earl Warren
28. D. John Sherman Cooper and Earl Warren
29. A. Gerald Ford

30. B. WC counsels
31. C. Richard Mosk
32. A. Burt Griffin
33. C. David Slawson
34. D. Howard Willens
35. B. Arlen Specter
36. B. Arlen Specter
37. D. William Coleman Jr.
38. B. David Belin and Howard Willens
39. D. William Coleman Jr.
40. D. Murray Laulicht
41. C. Alfredda Scobey
42. C. Sixteen
43. C. 88-202
44. C. 550
45. B. Marina Oswald
46. B. James Zahm
47. C. Avery Davis
48. D. Ralph Yarborough
49. A. Jean Hill
50. A. Mark Lane
51. B. Lyndon and Lady Bird Johnson
52. A. Sylvia Odio
53. D. Seventeen
54. B. Albert Bogard
55. B. Roy Kellerman
56. A. Douglas Dillon and Dean Rusk
57. B. Renatus Hartogs
58. A. Marina Oswald
59. B. Glen McBride
60. B. Robert Surrey
61. C. Harold Norman
62. A. Phillip Willis

63. B. Jim Wright
64. B. Darrell Tomlinson
65. A. J. C. Day
66. D. Howard Brennan
67. B. John Ready
68. A. Nelson Benton
69. A. Ruth Paine
70. D. S. M. Holland
71. B. Peter Gregory
72. B. Ten
73. D. George de Mohrenschildt
74. A. H. B. McLain
75. C. William Beavers
76. C. John Gallagher
77. A. Eight
78. C. 888
79. B. Oswald fired three shots from an Austrian-made rifle on the sixth floor of the TSBD
80. D. Secret Service protection methods should be reevaluated.
81. D. Twenty-six
82. A. 3154
83. A. II
84. C. No. 139
85. B. II, III, VII
86. A. No. 165
87. C. Volumes V and XIV
88. C. No. 324
89. C. IV
90. D. No. 197
91. D. He never testified
92. B. Nos. 344 to 346
93. A. B. H. Combest
94. A. Nos. 690 to 693
95. C. Fidel Castro

96. A. *The New York Times*
97. C. *Life Magazine*
98. D. 87 percent
99. B. 61 percent
100. A. National Archives

President Kennedy's limousine and the Secret Service follow-up car entering Dealey Plaza on Houston Street moments before the assassination. *Corbis / Getty Images*

As the motorcade passes the Texas School Book Depository on Elm Street, Secret Service Agents Tim McIntyre and John Ready react to the sound of rifle fire. *Corbis / Getty Images*

Police officers and Secret Service gather around JFK's limousine at Parkland Memorial Hospital. *Cecil Stoughton / John F. Kennedy Presidential Library and Museum.*

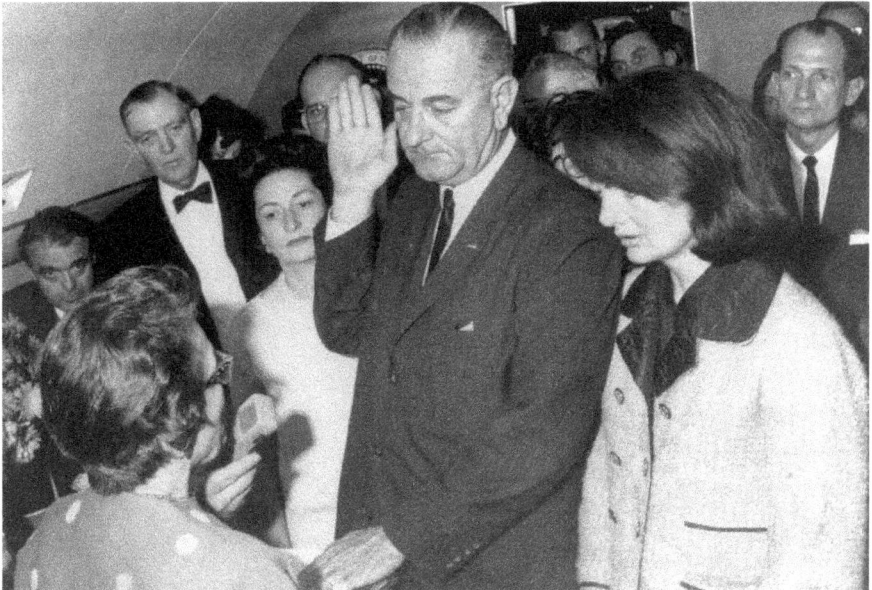

Vice President Lyndon B. Johnson takes the oath of office on *Air Force One* at Love Field in Dallas, following the assassination. *Bettmann / Getty Images*

The presumptive assassin, Lee Harvey Oswald is escorted through Dallas Police headquarters. He received a cut on his forehead in a scuffle with officers. *Bettmann / Getty Images*

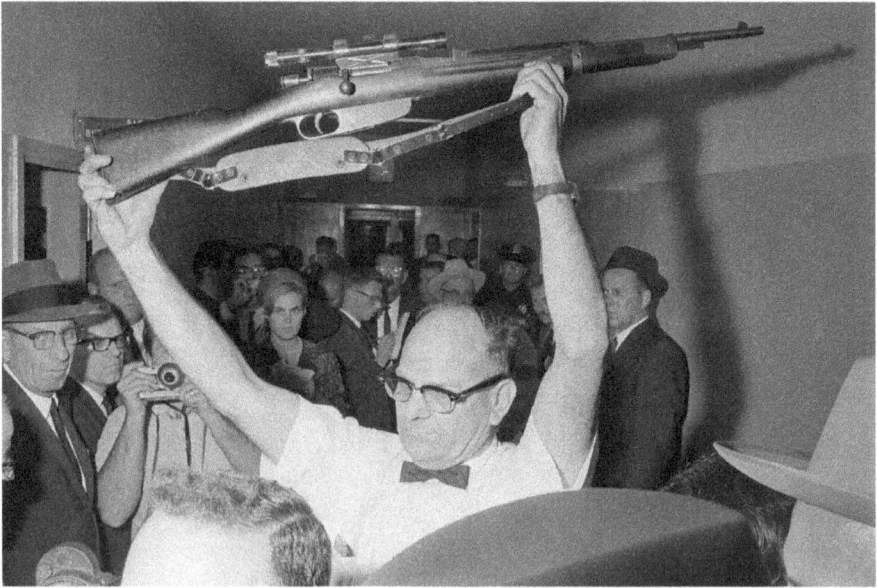

Dallas Police Lieutenant J.C. Day displays the rifle used in the assassination of President Kennedy and wounding of Governor Connally. *Bettmann / Getty Images*

A US Navy ambulance bearing the casket of the late President John F. Kennedy returns to the White House. *Robert Knudsen / John F. Kennedy Presidential Library and Museum*

On a solemn day in Washington, DC, JFK's funeral cortege passes mourners on its way to the US Capitol. *Reporters Associes / Getty Images*

THE GARRISON INVESTIGATION AND OTHER CONSPIRACY THEORIES

THE GARRISON INVESTIGATION

1. Earling (Jim) Garrison was born on November 20, 1921, in _____.
   A. Hays, Kansas
   B. Denison, Iowa
   C. Kearney, Nebraska
   D. Bozeman, Montana

2. The oldest son of Earling R. Garrison and Jane Anne Robinson, he was one of _____ children.
   A. two
   B. four
   C. seven
   D. eleven

3. At the age of four, young Earling decided to change his name to "Jimmy," in honor of the _____.
   A. butcher
   B. milkman
   C. paperboy
   D. babysitter

4. When Garrison turned six years old, his parents separated. Shortly thereafter, Mrs. Garrison and the children relocated to New Orleans. In which area of the city did they live?
   A. Gentilly
   B. Lakeview
   C. French Quarter
   D. Esplanade Ridge

5. Name the famous American playwright who was their neighbor.
   A. T. S. Eliot
   B. Arthur Miller
   C. Eugene O'Neill
   D. Tennessee Williams

6. As a single parent, how did Mrs. Garrison support her family?
   A. Cleaning houses
   B. Teaching school
   C. Grooming horses
   D. Selling insurance

7. In 1935, Garrison was enrolled in which high school?
   A. Edna Karr
   B. Alcee Fortier
   C. Bishop McManus
   D. St. Katherine Drexel

8. When America entered World War II, Garrison joined the US Army Air Corps, serving as a _____.
   A. navigator
   B. bombardier
   C. waist gunner
   D. reconnaissance pilot

9. Between 1943 and 1945, Garrison flew a total of _____ combat missions.
   A. eleven
   B. fifteen
   C. thirty-five
   D. forty-two

10. Near the end of the war, Garrison witnessed firsthand the atrocities committed against the Jews in this Nazi death camp.
    A. Dachau
    B. Treblinka
    C. Auschwitz
    D. Bergen-Belsen

11. In 1946, Garrison was unsuccessful in his attempt to reenlist due to demobilization. Returning to civilian life, he entered which of the following law schools?
    A. Tulane
    B. Loyola
    C. Stanford
    D. Georgetown

12. One of Garrison's law professors would later go on to serve as an assistant counsel on the Warren Commission. Who was he?
    A. Joseph Ball
    B. Leon Hubert
    C. Samuel Stern
    D. Albert Jenner

13. After graduating in 1949, Garrison joined the prestigious law firm of _____.
    A. Hubbard, Sisk, and Vance
    B. Nathan, Fishman, and Lilly
    C. Deutsch, Kerrigan, and Stiles
    D. Milner, Watkins, and Glenmore

14. Experiencing health issues, Garrison left the firm after less than a year and joined the FBI. To which city was he assigned?
    A. Butte, Montana
    B. Detroit, Michigan
    C. Las Vegas, Nevada
    D. Seattle, Washington

15. When the Korean War began in 1950, Garrison resigned from the FBI and was reactivated by the US Army. Where was he assigned and to which branch?
    A. Fort Dix, New Jersey / Infantry
    B. Fort Sill, Oklahoma / Field Artillery
    C. Fort Bragg, North Carolina / Airborne
    D. Fort Carson, Colorado / Communications

16. Suffering from symptoms of "battle fatigue," brought on by his experiences in World War II, Garrison was admitted to Brooke Army Hospital in Texas, where he was diagnosed with _____.
    A. paranoia
    B. agoraphobia
    C. schizophrenia
    D. hypochondriasis

17. Garrison's medical condition resulted in an honorable discharge from the US Army on _____.
    A. May 4, 1951
    B. June 8, 1951
    C. August 14, 1951
    D. October 31, 1951

18. Returning to New Orleans, Garrison was appointed _____ in 1952.
    A. assistant housing director
    B. deputy safety commissioner
    C. assistant recreation director
    D. deputy sanitation commissioner

19. In 1962, Garrison ran against and defeated the incumbent Richard Dowling to become district attorney of Orleans Parish. By how many votes did he win the election?
    A. 7,030
    B. 8,213
    C. 9,769
    D. 10,258

20. Which tactic did Garrison borrow from the JFK presidential campaign that helped to secure his victory?
    A. Fundraising
    B. Newsletters
    C. Endorsements
    D. TV commercials

21. Garrison's initial interest in the Kennedy assassination began on November 24, 1963, when he interviewed a private investigator named _____.
    A. Jack Martin
    B. Billy Hauser
    C. Ed Simmons
    D. Tim Lambert

22. The investigator told Garrison that a former airline pilot, right-wing sympathizer, and self-ordained priest named David Ferrie participated in the assassination. According to Martin, Ferrie _____.
    A. may have hypnotized Oswald into killing JFK
    B. was ordered to fly the assassin(s) out of Dallas
    C. knew Oswald when they were both members of the Civil Air Patrol
    D. All of the above

23. Ferrie was later found dead in his apartment in New Orleans. The cause of death was listed as a(n) _____.
    A. suicide
    B. heart attack
    C. cerebral hemorrhage
    D. accidental electrocution

24. In March of 1965, a Louisiana congressman encouraged Garrison to conduct his own investigation into the Kennedy assassination. Who was he?
    A. Hale Boggs
    B. James Morrison
    C. Overton Brooks
    D. Harold McSween

25. After reading the Warren Report and which of the following books did Garrison become convinced that JFK's death was the result of a conspiracy?
    A. *Case Closed*, *JFK in Dallas*, and *High Treason*
    B. *Whitewash*, *Rush to Judgement*, and *Inquest*
    C. *Six Seconds in Dallas*, *Inquest*, and *Who Killed JFK?*
    D. *On the Trail of the Assassins*, *Whitewash*, and *Oswald's Tale*

26. To conduct his investigation, Garrison assembled a staff known as the "The Smith Group." The name "Smith" was in reference to a character found in this George Orwell novel.
    A. *1984*
    B. *Animal Farm*
    C. *Burmese Days*
    D. *Shooting an Elephant*

27. In March of 1967, Garrison arrested and charged Clay Shaw, a New Orleans _____ with conspiracy in the death of President Kennedy.
    A. lawyer
    B. movie critic
    C. businessman
    D. university professor

28. Based on which of the following did Garrison connect Shaw to Lee Harvey Oswald?

A. Shaw and Oswald had served together in the US Marines Corps.

B. Following his arrest, Oswald phoned Shaw from police headquarters.

C. Prior to the assassination, Shaw and Oswald were seen having dinner at Jack Ruby's nightclub.

D. One day after the assassination, Shaw, using the alias "Clay Bertrand," allegedly asked a lawyer named Dean Andrews to represent Oswald.

29. Garrison theorized that Shaw, Ferrie, Oswald, and an ex-FBI agent and private investigator named _____ were involved in an elaborate plot to kill Kennedy.

A. Luis Stolla

B. Guy Banister

C. Harold Snyder

D. Boris Durango

30. According to Garrison, the conspirators were acting on behalf of the _____.

A. CIA and Cuban exiles

B. FBI and Texas businessmen

C. Mafia and Lyndon Johnson

D. Soviet Union and Fidel Castro

31. Which role did Oswald allegedly play in the assassination?

A. Patsy

B. Decoy

C. Assassin

D. Getaway driver

32. Initially, the news media was intrigued by Garrison's inquiry, but as reporters delved more deeply, they discovered that his facts and sources were unreliable. Which magazine was one of the first to question Garrison's credibility?
    A. *Time*
    B. *Newsweek*
    C. *Atlantic Monthly*
    D. *Saturday Evening Post*

33. The most damning assault on Garrison's investigation came from a TV special entitled: _____.
    A. "NBC White Paper: The Garrison Hoax"
    B. "JFK's Assassination: Garrison's Deception"
    C. "Reasonable Doubt: Jim Garrison's Hypocrisy"
    D. "The JFK Conspiracy: The Case of Jim Garrison"

34. On the program, anchorman Frank McGee questioned whether Garrison was using witnesses that had perjured themselves during a pretrial hearing. Who were they?
    A. Perry Russo and Vernon Bundy
    B. John Mecham and Charles Fischer
    C. Butch Watson and Steve Alexander
    D. Miguel Torres and Johnny Bradshaw

35. Given equal airtime by NBC, Garrison accused the national media, in general, of withholding from the American people all the following information *except* _____.
    A. Oswald's prints were not found on the gun
    B. members of the WC covered up a conspiracy involving the CIA
    C. nitrate tests indicated that Oswald had not fired a rifle that day
    D. an overwhelming number of witnesses testified that shots had come from the grassy knoll

36. On whose late-night talk show was Garrison invited to discuss the case?
    A. Jack Paar
    B. Merv Griffin
    C. Johnny Carson
    D. Geraldo Rivera

37. Some fourteen months after Shaw was arrested, the trial began on _____.
    A. January 15, 1969
    B. January 23, 1969
    C. January 29, 1969
    D. January 31, 1969

38. How many men and how many women served on the jury?
    A. Six men and six women
    B. Ten men and two women
    C. Nine men and three women
    D. The jury was comprised of all men.

39. Who was the presiding judge?
    A. David Harris
    B. Joseph Anderson
    C. Edward Haggerty
    D. Matthew Johnson

40. All of the following lawyers served on Shaw's defense team except _____.
    A. F. Irvin Dymond
    B. Charles Campbell
    C. Salvatore Panzeca
    D. Edward Wegmann

41. To help prove Garrison's conspiracy theory, this piece of evidence was shown to the jury. It was the first time it had been seen in public.
    A. The Zapruder film
    B. JFK's autopsy report
    C. The assassination rifle
    D. Photos of the sniper's nest

42. Who was the only Kennedy autopsist to testify at the trial?
    A. Major Bennett Marco, USA
    B. Commander James Humes, USN
    C. Lieutenant Colonel Pierre Finck, USA
    D. Commander J. Thornton Boswell, USN

43. On March 1, 1969, following a brief deliberation, Shaw was acquitted. How long did it take the jury to render a decision?
    A. Twelve minutes
    B. Nineteen minutes
    C. Forty-one minutes
    D. Fifty-four minutes

44. Five years after the Shaw trial, Garrison was charged, tried, and found not guilty of _____.
    A. extortion
    B. embezzlement
    C. accepting bribes
    D. money laundering

45. Before his death, Shaw was involved in a multimillion-dollar lawsuit against Garrison and an organization of businessmen that had funded his investigation. What was it called?
    A. The Alliance for Right
    B. Citizens for Equal Justice
    C. Truth and Consequences Inc.
    D. Coalition of Concerned Americans

46. Maintaining his innocence to the very end, Shaw died of (a) _____ in
    1974.
    A. stroke
    B. lung cancer
    C. heart disease
    D. spinal meningitis

47. That same year, Garrison was replaced as New Orleans district attorney by
    the father of which actor and recording artist?
    A. Steve Tyrell
    B. Josh Groban
    C. Harry Connick
    D. Michael Bublé

48. In 1979, a former CIA director testified under oath that, at one time, Clay
    Shaw had provided information to the agency regarding his travels in Latin
    America. Who was he?
    A. John McCone
    B. Richard Helms
    C. William Casey
    D. James Schlesinger

49. The only man to bring criminal charges in the death of President John F.
    Kennedy, Garrison died of (a) _____ at the age of seventy in 1992.
    A. stroke
    B. cancer
    C. heart disease
    D. diabetic shock

OTHER CONSPIRACY THEORIES

50. Why do some researchers suspect that the US Secret Service was involved in the death of President Kennedy?
    A. Only one agent reacted to the gunfire.
    B. JFK's driver did not accelerate after the first shot.
    C. No agents were stationed in the high-rise buildings along the motorcade route.
    D. All of the above

51. According to this dubious theory, a Dallas Police officer named Roscoe White was one of three men who took part in the assassination of JFK. What were their alleged codenames?
    A. "Mercury," "Apollo," and "Gemini"
    B. "Lebanon," "Mandarin," and "Saul"
    C. "Swordfish," "Badger," and "Jackal"
    D. "Unicorn," "Lizard," and "Dragonfly"

52. Which statement, by Parkland Hospital's Dr. Malcolm Perry, led to speculation of more than one gunman in Dealey Plaza?
    A. There was an entrance wound above JFK's right ear.
    B. The wound in JFK's throat appeared to be an entrance wound.
    C. There was no evidence to suggest that JFK had been shot from behind.
    D. The number of wounds sustained by JFK strongly suggested that there were at least two assassins.

53. Name the Argentinian-born double agent who reportedly organized the military-style operation to assassinate President Kennedy.
    A. Luis Aguilar
    B. Rene Dussaq
    C. Miguel Caserio
    D. Jorge Barrancos

54. Although not commonly accepted, this theory contends that the government of South Vietnam was behind the assassination because _____.
    A. Kennedy was viewed as too weak on Communism
    B. Kennedy planned to withdraw all US forces from Vietnam by 1964
    C. Kennedy had ordered the assassination of its president, Ngo Dinh Diem
    D. Kennedy threatened to sign a separate peace agreement with North Vietnam

55. Which of the following is / are the reason(s) why the Mafia is suspected of killing JFK?
    A. Joseph Kennedy Sr. double-crossed the Mafia when he promised Sam Giancana that a Kennedy administration would take a hands-off approach to organized crime in exchange for their "assistance" in carrying the state of Illinois.
    B. Under Attorney General Robert Kennedy, the Justice Department mounted an unprecedented assault against organized crime.
    C. Fidel Castro's overthrow of the Batista government in 1959 and the US government's failed coup attempt in 1961 cost the Mafia millions in revenue.
    D. All of the above

56. According to a 1966 FBI memo, the KGB theorized that President Kennedy had been the victim of a well-organized plot—possibly involving _____.
    A. Malcolm X
    B. Allen Dulles
    C. Richard Nixon
    D. Lyndon Johnson

57. In its final report, the HSCA could not rule out the possibility that individual members of the_____ played a role in JFK's murder.
    A. KGB
    B. Mafia
    C. Ku Klux Klan
    D. Dallas Police

58. Which of the 486 frames of the Zapruder film do conspiracy buffs point to as evidence of a second shooter?
    A. 313–316
    B. 318–321
    C. 347–350
    D. 361–364

59. This theory asserts that a rogue element within the US government carried out the assassination of JFK because he threatened to expose the existence of extraterrestrials. What was this "Deep State" faction called?
    A. Fab Four
    B. Colossus Six
    C. Majestic Twelve
    D. Rainbow Eighteen

60. Who was the Cuban intelligence officer that allegedly knew Oswald and praised his marksmanship?
    A. Ramiro Jesus Abreu Quintana
    B. Bembe Alvaro Camilo Alvarez
    C. Dalian Emeterio Anton Garcia
    D. Gimoaldo Homero Eterio Perez

61. According to Jerome Kroth, a psychology professor and author of *Conspiracy in Camelot*, there wasn't one assassin in Dealey Plaza, but _____.
    A. eight
    B. twelve
    C. nineteen
    D. twenty-seven

62. Shortly before his death in 1976, mobster Johnny Roselli purportedly told legendary investigative journalist _____ that the Kennedy assassination was planned and carried out by the Cuban government and organized crime.
   A. Bill O'Reilly
   B. Drew Pearson
   C. Jack Anderson
   D. Walter Winchell

63. In a photograph by assassination witness Mary Moorman, researcher Gary Mack discovered what appears to be a shadowy figure behind the picket fence on the grassy knoll. In conspiracy circles he is referred to as _____.
   A. "Badge Man"
   B. "Ghost Man"
   C. "Uniform Man"
   D. "Secret Agent Man"

64. Name the Cuban rebel leader, known as "El Mexicano," who may have consorted with Oswald prior to November 22, 1963.
   A. Bembe Alejandro Diaz
   B. Castilo Desiderio Lopez
   C. Emeterio Filiberto Alvarez
   D. Francisco Rodriguez Tamayo

65. According to a declassified CIA document, an unnamed individual phoned US authorities in Canberra, Australia, on November 23, 1963, and discussed the possibility that Soviet officials had financed President Kennedy's assassination. Who did he claim to be?
   A. A Soviet defector living in Sydney
   B. A British naval attaché stationed in Perth
   C. A French engineer vacationing in Melbourne
   D. A Polish chauffer at the Soviet embassy in Canberra

66. In 1981, this conspiracy theory was debunked following the exhumation of Oswald's remains?

A. JFK was assassinated by a Soviet imposter.

B. Oswald's body had been stolen by grave robbers.

C. A look-alike Oswald was hired by the CIA to kill JFK.

D. Oswald was programmed to assassinate JFK by the Chinese.

67. Name the federal agency tasked with tracking down all leads in the days and weeks following the assassination.

A. FBI

B. US Marshals

C. Secret Service

D. Federal Protective Service

68. Which US president suspected Fidel Castro of ordering President Kennedy's murder?

A. Jimmy Carter

B. Barack Obama

C. Ronald Reagan

D. Lyndon Johnson

69. This Louisiana crime boss had the motive, the means, and the opportunity to have JFK assassinated after his deportation to Guatemala in 1961.

A. Carlos Marcello

B. Joseph Gagliano

C. Sylvestro Carollo

D. Charles Matranga

70. Whom did French President Charles de Gaulle believe was behind the Kennedy assassination?

A. Dallas Police

B. Ku Klux Klan

C. Richard Nixon

D. J. Edgar Hoover

71. Following November 22, 1963, Fidel Castro's two greatest fears were that ___.
    A. he would be blamed, and the US would invade Cuba
    B. Cuba would be blockaded, and he would be imprisoned
    C. Fulgencio Batista would return to power, and he would be executed
    D. the Soviet Union would withdraw its support, and he would be overthrown

72. Which of the following authors is credited with being the first to implicate Lyndon Johnson in Kennedy's assassination?
    A. Sylvia Meagher
    B. Joachim Joesten
    C. Anthony Summers
    D. Thomas Buchanan

73. According to the "Illuminati theory," Kennedy was murdered because he tried to control the power of the _____.
    A. Federal Reserve
    B. Treasury Department
    C. Internal Revenue System
    D. Securities and Exchange Commission

74. In November of 2021, members of this far-right conspiracy cult claimed that JFK would reappear in Dallas and announce the reinstatement of President Donald Trump.
    A. QAnon
    B. Proud Boys
    C. Hammerskins
    D. Sons of Justice

75. Who was the White House "plumber" that allegedly made a deathbed confession implicating the CIA in JFK's murder?
    A. Frank Sturgis
    B. Howard Hunt
    C. Gordon Liddy
    D. James McCord

76. The "Umbrella Man," a perennial favorite of conspiracy theorists, was mistakenly thought to have signaled Kennedy's killers when he raised and lowered his "bumbershoot" as the presidential limousine passed the TSBD. Appearing before the HSCA in 1978, he claimed that it was his way of protesting Joseph Kennedy Sr's support for Britain's appeasement of Nazi Germany. What was the "Umbrella Man's" actual name?
    A. Louie Steven Witt
    B. Jameson Paul Bailey
    C. Brian David Harrison
    D. Charles Joseph McIntyre

77. Which big-city district attorney once calculated that a minimum of eighty assassins had been accused in various conspiracy scenarios?
    A. Gil Garcetti
    B. Frank Hogan
    C. Vincent Bugliosi
    D. William Overton

78. According to documents released in 2017, Kremlin leaders were convinced that JFK's murder was orchestrated by _____.
    A. right-wing extremists
    B. organized crime bosses
    C. US intelligence agencies
    D. officials in the Kennedy administration

79. Before his death in 1987, he reportedly confessed his involvement in the Kennedy assassination to lawyer Frank Ragano. Who was he?
    A. Jack Ruby
    B. Clay Shaw
    C. Fidel Castro
    D. Santos Trafficante

80. Initially considered suspects, the _____ (identified as Gus Adams, Harold Doyle, and John Gedney) were discovered in the railyard behind the grassy knoll shortly after the shooting. Taken into custody by Dallas Police, the men were questioned and released four days later.
    A. "Three Stooges"
    B. "Three Amigos"
    C. "Three Tramps"
    D. "Three Vagabonds"

81. This "Non-Conspiracy Theory" may be too inane to mention, but I will anyway. In _____, author Jim Moore postulated that Oswald demonstrated evidence of guilt when, after the assassination, he purchased a Coca-Cola instead of his usual Dr. Pepper.
    A. *Dallas 1963*
    B. *Conspiracy of One*
    C. *Oswald Acted Alone*
    D. *The Oswald Conspiracy*

82. Which former US president called for the abolishment of the CIA one month after the death of JFK?
    A. Harry Truman
    B. Herbert Hoover
    C. Franklin Roosevelt
    D. Dwight Eisenhower

83. A Cuban exile with connections to US intelligence agencies, he allegedly confided in his sons that he was Lee Harvey Oswald's sniper instructor.
    A. Juan "Jackal" Lopez
    B. Fernando "Rat" Rubio
    C. Tomas "Tiger" Rodriguez
    D. Ricardo "Monkey" Morales

84. In *Appointment in Dallas: The Final Solution to the Assassination of JFK,* former Los Angeles police officer and author Hugh McDonald claimed that a Soviet assassin was contracted by the KGB to murder Kennedy. Who was he?
    A. Georgi Visko
    B. Igor Sarkinov
    C. Sasha Retinski
    D. Andrei Copolev

85. According to author Priscilla Johnson McMillan, the reason why JFK conspiracy theories are so prevalent is because _____ [27]
    A. "people have nothing better to do or to think about."
    B. "people like to live vicariously through their heroes and villains."
    C. "people need a form of escapism and after all everyone loves a mystery."
    D. "people cannot accept the disparity between the magnitude of the deed and the insignificance of the perpetrator."

86. Name the labor union official, with underworld connections, who purportedly delivered three high-powered rifles to Dallas prior to the assassination.
    A. Bing Myers
    B. Paul Carlton
    C. Frank Sheeran
    D. Gerald O'Toole

87. Which JFK researcher believes that the Zapruder film may have been altered by the CIA, and thus is proof of a government plot?
    A. David Lifton
    B. Roger Smythe
    C. Harrison Carter
    D. William Wyman

88. In a 2013 interview, US Secretary of State _____ said he had "serious doubts that Oswald acted alone."[28]
    A. John Kerry
    B. Colin Powell
    C. Rex Tillerson
    D. Warren Christopher

89. Which radio personality contended that Kennedy was killed by a "gas pressure device" supplied by aliens from outer space?
    A. Glen Beck
    B. Jerry Doyle
    C. Rush Limbaugh
    D. Milton William Cooper

90. In the closing hours of its investigation, the HSCA determined that the assassination was "probably" the result of a conspiracy. This conclusion was based in part on _____.
    A. a home movie of Lee Harvey Oswald meeting with Jack Ruby the day before JFK was assassinated
    B. a dictabelt recording of what sounded like four shots fired as the motorcade passed through Dealey Plaza
    C. a grainy photograph of what appeared to be an assassin in the fifth-floor window of the Dal-Tex Building
    D. a signed confession from a convicted felon who claimed that he was the second shooter on the third floor of the TSBD

91. Over the years, all of the following allegations have been made regarding a possible Tippit-Oswald connection *except* _____.
    A. Tippit was ordered to kill Oswald
    B. Tippit was Oswald's getaway driver
    C. Tippit purchased the rifle used by Oswald
    D. Tippit had a chance encounter with Oswald

92. According to a 2015 article in *Politico Magazine,* this former CIA chief was involved in a "benign cover-up" to withhold information from the Warren Commission regarding US attempts to eliminate Fidel Castro.[29]
    A. Porter Goss
    B. Allen Dulles
    C. Walter Smith
    D. John McCone

93. Name the conspiracist who hypothesized that high-ranking Dallas Police officials were involved in the assassination.
    A. Stew Vinson
    B. Dalton Ward
    C. Harrison Martin
    D. Richard Gilbride

94. This convicted hitman and father of a well-known TV and movie actor once professed to be JFK's killer.
    A. Kyle Smith
    B. Carson Dafoe
    C. George Baldwin
    D. Charles Harrelson

95. A known prostitute and drug addict, she told authorities that on November 20, 1963, she was in the company of two men who were on their way to kill President Kennedy. In the summer of 1965, her lifeless body was found on a highway near Big Sandy, Texas. What was her name?
    A. Joy Dale
    B. Nancy Myers
    C. Rose Cheramie
    D. Lucinda Stafford

96. Who was the former CIA director that asserted in his 2021 book that Oswald was acting at the behest of the Soviet Union when he murdered JFK?
A. David Petraeus
B. George Tenent
C. James Woosley
D. Michael Hayden

97. Name the 2016 presidential candidate who said, "All I did is point out the fact that on the cover of the *National Enquirer* there was a picture of him [Ted Cruz's father] and crazy Lee Harvey Oswald having breakfast."[30]
A. Jeb Bush
B. Chris Christie
C. Donald Trump
D. Michael Bloomberg

98. Why do people continue to doubt that Oswald acted alone?
A. No one saw him shoot the president.
B. He was in the second-floor lunchroom at the time of the assassination.
C. People cannot accept that a man like Oswald could commit such an act.
D. A and C

99. According to the "Military-Industrial Complex" theory, Kennedy was eliminated because he _____.
A. planned to slash military spending
B. threatened to fire the Joint Chiefs of Staff
C. planned a total US withdrawal from Vietnam
D. ordered the reduction in the number US nuclear weapons

100. Which famous piece of evidence do conspiracy theorists often point to in support of a second shooter on the grassy knoll?
A. A bullet entered the right side of JFK's neck.
B. The final shot caused JFK's head to move back and to the left.
C. Governor Connally had a small entrance wound in his right shoulder.
D. In Zapruder frames 415–426, the presidential limousine swerves to the left.

CHAPTER SIX ANSWERS

1. B. Denison, Iowa
2. A. two
3. C. paperboy
4. C. French Quarter
5. D. Tennessee Williams
6. D. Selling insurance
7. B. Alcee Fortier
8. D. reconnaissance pilot
9. C. thirty-five
10. A. Dachau
11. A. Tulane
12. B. Leon Hubert
13. C. Deutsch, Kerrigan, and Stiles
14. D. Seattle, Washington
15. B. Fort Sill, Oklahoma / Field Artillery
16. D. hypochondriasis
17. D. October 31, 1951
18. B. deputy safety commissioner
19. A. 7,030
20. D. TV commercials
21. A. Jack Martin
22. D. All of the above
23. C. cerebral hemorrhage
24. A. Hale Boggs
25. B. *Whitewash*, *Rush to Judgement*, and *Inquest*
26. A. *1984*
27. C. businessman
28. D. One day after the assassination, Shaw, using the alias "Clay Bertrand," allegedly asked a lawyer named Dean Andrews to represent Oswald.
29. B. Guy Banister

30.   A. CIA and Cuban exiles
31.   A. Patsy
32.   D. *Saturday Evening Post*
33.   D. "The JFK Conspiracy: The Case of Jim Garrison"
34.   A. Perry Russo and Vernon Bundy
35.   B. members of the WC covered-up a conspiracy involving the CIA
36.   C. Johnny Carson
37.   C. January 29, 1969
38.   D. The jury was comprised of all men.
39.   C. Edward Haggerty
40.   B. Charles Campbell
41.   A. The Zapruder film
42.   C. Lieutenant Colonel Pierre Finck, USA
43.   D. Fifty-four minutes
44.   C. accepting bribes
45.   C. Truth and Consequences Inc.
46.   B. lung cancer
47.   C. Harry Connick
48.   B. Richard Helms
49.   B. cancer
50.   D. All of the above
51.   B. "Lebanon," "Mandarin," and "Saul"
52.   B. The wound in JFK's throat appeared to be an entrance wound.
53.   B. Rene Dussaq
54.   C. Kennedy had ordered the assassination of its president, Ngo Dinh Diem
55.   D. All of the above
56.   D. Lyndon Johnson
57.   B. Mafia
58.   A. 313–316
59.   C. Majestic Twelve
60.   A. Ramiro Jesus Abreu Quintana
61.   D. twenty-seven
62.   C. Jack Anderson

63. A. "Badge Man"
64. D. Francisco Rodriguez Tamayo
65. D. A Polish chauffer at the Soviet embassy in Canberra
66. A. JFK was assassinated by a Soviet imposter.
67. A. FBI
68. D. Lyndon Johnson
69. A. Carlos Marcello
70. A. Dallas Police
71. A. he would be blamed, and the US would invade Cuba
72. B. Joachim Joesten
73. A. Federal Reserve
74. A. QAnon
75. B. Howard Hunt
76. A. Louie Steven Witt
77. C. Vincent Bugliosi
78. A. right-wing extremists
79. D. Santos Trafficante
80. C. "Three Tramps"
81. B. *Conspiracy of One*
82. A. Harry Truman
83. D. Ricardo "Monkey" Morales
84. A. Georgi Visko
85. D. "people cannot accept the disparity between the magnitude of the deed and the insignificance of the perpetrator."
86. C. Frank Sheeran
87. A. David Lifton
88. A. John Kerry
89. D. Milton William Cooper
90. B. a dictabelt recording of what sounded like four shots fired as the motorcade passed through Dealey Plaza
91. C. Tippit purchased the rifle used by Oswald
92. D. John McCone
93. D. Richard Gilbride
94. D. Charles Harrelson

95. C. Rose Cheramie
96. C. James Woosley
97. C. Donald Trump
98. D. A and C
99. C. planned a total US withdrawal from Vietnam
100. B. The final shot caused JFK's head to move back and to the left.

CHAPTER SEVEN

IN THEIR OWN WORDS

1. "Here is a bulletin from CBS News: In Dallas, Texas, three shots were fired at President Kennedy's motorcade in downtown Dallas. The first reports say that President Kennedy has been seriously wounded by this shooting."[31]
   A. Bill Shadel
   B. Roger Mudd
   C. Walter Cronkite
   D. Terry Drinkwater

2. "These details about the same as previously. President Kennedy shot today just as his motorcade left downtown Dallas. Mrs. Kennedy jumped up and grabbed Mr. Kennedy, she called, 'Oh, no!' The motorcade sped on."[32]
   A. David Brinkley
   B. Walter Cronkite
   C. Douglas Edwards
   D. Howard K. Smith

3. "From Dallas, Texas, the flash, apparently official. President Kennedy died at 1:00 p.m. Central Standard Time. Two o'clock Eastern Standard Time, some thirty-eight minutes ago... Vice President Johnson has left the hospital in Dallas, but we do not know to where he has proceeded. Presumably, he will be taking the oath of office shortly and become the 36th president of the United States."[33]
   A. Chet Huntley
   B. Frank Reynolds
   C. Harry Reasoner
   D. Walter Cronkite

4. "The immediate sense of personal loss is much greater for the American people than it was at the death of McKinley, Garfield, and even Lincoln because by means of television the president was almost a daily visitor in our homes."[34]
   A. Pope Paul VI
   B. Billy Graham
   C. Martin Luther King
   D. Bishop Fulton J. Sheen

5. "My first impression was that the shots came from the right and overhead, but I also had a fleeting impression that the noise appeared to come from the front in the area of the triple overpass."[35]
   A. Gary Raffa
   B. Dave Powers
   C. Ralph Dungan
   D. Harris Wofford

6. "The Kennedy assassination became the template for coverage…We were working in one of the worst moments of the nation's life back then and we didn't know what to make of it, much like what happened on 9/11."[36]
   A. Bob Schieffer
   B. Bill Lawrence
   C. John Chancellor
   D. Heywood Hale Broun

7. "If I had to do it over again, I would have stayed 1,000 miles away from Dallas that day."[37]
   A. Royce Skelton
   B. Abraham Zapruder
   C. Buell Wesley Frazier
   D. James Thomas Aycox

8. "As soon as the President was pronounced dead, the Secret Service more or less—well, requested that we clear the room and leave them with the President's body, which was done. Everything that the Secret Service wished was carried out."[38]
   A. Red Duke
   B. Charles Baxter
   C. Joseph Goldstrich
   D. Charles Crenshaw

9. "I saw one man run towards the passenger cars on the railroad siding after the volley of shots…He had something in his hand."[39]
   A. E. W. Rey
   B. J. C. Price
   C. B. W. Jones
   D. S. M. Holland

10. "We can't accept very comfortably that two nobodies, two nothings—Lee Harvey Oswald and Jack Ruby—were able to change the course of world history."[40]
    A. Ron McAlister
    B. Jimmy Darnell
    C. Robert Jackson
    D. Hugh Aynesworth

11. "As the motorcade was approximately one-third of the way to the underpass, traveling between ten and fifteen miles per hour, I heard a loud noise."[41]
    A. Clint Hill
    B. Jerry Kivett
    C. Gerald Behn
    D. William Greer

12. "You stay with the President. I'm taking some of my men for Johnson."[42]
   A. Floyd Boring
   B. Emory Roberts
   C. J. Walter Coughlin
   D. Dennis Halterman

13. "The President was on a stretcher. His arms were out on arm boards like this and Dr. Carrico, who was a second-year resident was trying to put a tube into his windpipe and then the tracheal tube to get an airway established, but the president was motionless..."[43]
   A. Ben Wilson
   B. Paul Peters
   C. Ronald Jones
   D. Malcolm Perry

14. "It's natural that an event like this would cause skepticism and suspicions, especially in light of what has come out about our government."[44]
   A. Leon Hubert
   B. Richard Mosk
   C. Francis Adams
   D. David Slawson

15. "Why did they kill Uncle Jack?"[45]
   A. Rory Kennedy
   B. Kerry Kennedy
   C. David A. Kennedy
   D. Christopher G. Kennedy

16. "As the first gunshot sounded, I looked up to the building, thinking somebody was throwing firecrackers out of the window, but I only had a split second before some stranger, and I still don't know who it was, pulled me to the ground."[46]
    A. Tina Towner
    B. Linda Wilding
    C. Becky Wilcox
    D. Gayle Newman

17. "My own feeling was that Bobby was worried that there might be some conspiracy and that it might be his fault..."[47]
    A. Edward Kennedy
    B. Robert McNamara
    C. Nicholas Katzenbach
    D. Llewellyn Thompson

18. "It is important to know who killed Jack Kennedy and why."[48]
    A. Joe Biden
    B. Earl Warren
    C. Jim Garrison
    D. Richard Nixon

19. "At that time it seemed like the activity was centered around the Texas School Book Depository, so, that is when I heard someone say, one of the sergeants or lieutenants, I don't know, 'Don't let anyone out of the Texas School Book Depository,' and so, I went to a gap that had not been filled, which was at the southwest corner."[49]
    A. Bobby Hargis
    B. Rodney Smart
    C. Douglas Jackson
    D. Harold Freeman

20. "We had no idea the President was going to the hospital. When we got there, we were permitted to run up next to his car...It was a horrific sight. I will never forget it."[50]
    A. Bob Clark
    B. Steve Bell
    C. Ron Cochran
    D. John Chancellor

21. "The enormous interest in the [Kennedy] assassination, and the persistence of conspiracy theories behind it, is yet more evidence of the power of Kennedy's posthumous life."[51]
    A. Robert Caro
    B. Alan Brinkley
    C. Michael Beschloss
    D. Arthur Schlesinger Jr.

22. "A gentleman [Oswald] walked in the door and walked up and introduced himself to me and tells me he wants to look at a car. I show him a car on the showroom floor, and take him for a ride out Stemmons Expressway and back, and he was driving at 60 to 70 miles an hour and came back to the showroom...And the day that the President was shot, when I heard that—they had the radio on in the showroom, and when I heard the name, that he had shot a policeman over in Oak Cliff, I pulled out some business cards that I had wrote his name on the back on, and said, 'He won't be a prospect anymore because he is going to jail...'" [52]
    A. Bill O'Leary
    B. Albert Bogard
    C. Delbert Stimes
    D. Tim Waterman

23. "It looked as though the entire city had turned up. It was really great. Dallas had shown that it really loved that president."[53]
    A. Edwin Lee
    B. Ken Albert
    C. Simon Ross
    D. Bob Huffaker

24. "Now his brother was dead. And in the barrage of phone calls and conversations on November 22, it is clear to see where Bobby was hunting for the culprits…"[54]
    A. David Talbot
    B. A. Scott Berg
    C. Vernon Bogdanor
    D. Margaret McMillan

25. "I have a great deal of guilt about that. Had I turned in a different direction, I'd have made it. It's my fault…And I'll live with that to my grave."[55]
    A. Clint Hill
    B. Lem Johns
    C. Paul Burns
    D. Andrew Berger

26. "What really worries me is that I hope they've got tight security around Lee Harvey Oswald."[56]
    A. Dean Rusk
    B. Stewart Udall
    C. Orville Freeman
    D. Robert McNamara

27. "The President was nonchalant about his own security. In the Southern sunshine and warm temperatures, he had the protective bubble of his blue Lincoln limousine removed and the bullet-proof side windows rolled down."[57]
A. T. D. Smythe
B. Carlton Wilson
C. Richard Reeves
D. Michael O'Brien

28. "He said when the first shot was fired, he glanced back and there was something in the building [TSBD], he couldn't determine what it was, but it was just something there that he couldn't explain, but he was definite that the shots did come from there."[58]
A. E. D. Brewer
B. Bobby Hargis
C. D. V. Harkness
D. Clyde Haygood

29. "Did the FBI or any other investigatory agency of the Government ever show you a picture of the rifle that was supposed to have been used to assassinate the President?"[59]
A. Burt Griffin
B. Samuel Stern
C. Albert Jenner
D. Wesley Liebeler

30. "The dark stocky man [Jack Ruby] with the hat on…put the gun right in his belly. One of the wildest scenes I have ever seen…The man rushed up and jammed the gun right into Oswald's stomach and fired one shot…"[60]
A. Sid Davis
B. Ike Pappas
C. George Herman
D. Howard K. Smith

31. "All of a sudden someone [Jack Ruby] stepped out from the right, and the thought flashed in my mind, 'He's blocking my view!'"[61]
   A. Jim McCoy
   B. Tom Dillard
   C. Bob Jackson
   D. Allen Mitchell

32. "While the nation was grieving around its television sets, we were there on the scene reporting, unable to take out time to grieve or to even know what was being done in Washington DC, the ceremony, the funeral, and the sadness that the other people were living through their television sets. We who were broadcasting didn't see it all."[62]
   A. James Weiss
   B. Marty Cohen
   C. Bob Huffaker
   D. Keith Meyers

33. "They killed him, they killed him!"[63]
   A. Marilyn Sitzman
   B. Abraham Zapruder
   C. Bonnie Sutherland
   D. Elizabeth Thompson

34. "I don't care about who the shooters were. I care about who the planners were."[64]
   A. Jim Garrison
   B. Dave Powers
   C. J. Edgar Hoover
   D. Robert Kennedy

35. "They do love this president, don't they?"[65]
   A. Liz Carpenter
   B. Helen Thomas
   C. Gloria Emerson
   D. Barbara Walters

36. "I saw a squad car, and by that time there was four or five people that had gathered, a couple of cars had stopped. Then I saw—I went on up to the squad car and saw the police officer [Tippit] lying in the street. I see he had been shot in the head. So, the first thing I did, I ran over to the squad car. I didn't know whether anybody reported it or not. So, I got on the police radio and called them, and told them a man had been shot, told them the location, I thought the officer was dead."[66]
A. Mary Brock
B. Clem Davison
C. Kate Bellman
D. Ted Callaway

37. "He [President Kennedy] appeared to be terminal, if not already expired, and Dr. Carrico said that he had seen some attempted respirations, agonal respirations, and with that history, we went ahead with emergency measures to try to restore the airway."[67]
A. Tom Shires
B. Ronald Jones
C. Malcolm Perry
D. Charles Crenshaw

38. "With all the troubles we've had since Kennedy was killed, I think people respect him all the more."[68]
A. Paul Newman
B. Sidney Poitier
C. Marlon Brando
D. Cliff Robertson

39. "It sounded like they [shots] were right there more or less like motorcycle backfire, but I thought that they were these dumb balls that they throw at the cement because I could see the smoke coming up off the cement."[69]
A. Frank Reilly
B. Austin Miller
C. Royce Skelton
D. James Hodges

40. "And then the thing that happened then was a loud shot—first I thought they were saluting the President, somebody—even maybe a motorcycle backfire…Well, the first shot—I really did not pay any attention to it, because I did not know what was happening. The second shot, it sounded like it was right in the building [TSBD], the second and third shot. And it sounded—it even shook the building, the side we were on. Cement fell on my head."[70]
    A. Tyrone Miller
    B. James Jarman
    C. Sylvester Quigley
    D. Bonnie Ray Williams

41. "I'll tell you something that will rock you…Kennedy was trying to get Castro, but Castro got to him first."[71]
    A. Bob Dylan
    B. Frank Sinatra
    C. Barry Goldwater
    D. Lyndon Johnson

42. "And I remember glancing up to a window on the far right, which at the time impressed me as the sixth or seventh floor and seeing about a foot of a rifle being—the barrel brought into the window."[72]
    A. Kent Biffle
    B. Malcolm Couch
    C. Ted Rozumalski
    D. Mary Rice Brogan

43. "I heard an explosion which I made the comment that I believe, in my memory, I believe I said, 'My God, they've thrown a torpedo,' and why I said 'torpedo,' I don't know…"[73]
    A. Tom Dillard
    B. George Venuto
    C. Anthony Comer
    D. Bob Worthington

44. "Well, when I heard the first shot it was too loud to be a firecracker, I knew that, because there was quite a big boom, and I don't know, just out of nowhere, I looked up like that, just straight up."[74]
    A. Virgil Foster
    B. James Worrell
    C. Arch Harrington
    D. Carl Martienssen

45. "I was of the opinion, or perhaps expressed, either by Mr. Kelley or Mr. Mike Howard, that had we been placed in a room facing each other, perhaps more could have been learned or something could have been learned about whether or not he [Oswald] was actually guilty or how much he was involved in the assassination of the President of the United States."[75]
    A. Robert Oswald
    B. Marina Oswald
    C. William Oswald
    D. Marguerite Oswald

46. "What made me almost certain that the shot came from behind was because at the time I was looking at the President, just as he was struck, it caused him to move a bit forward…"[76]
    A. Mike Quinn
    B. Larry Grove
    C. James Altgens
    D. Harry Cabluck

47. "I thought it was firecrackers or somebody celebrating the arrival of the President. It didn't occur to me at first what had happened until this Gloria came running up to us and told us the President had been shot."[77]
    A. Billy Lovelady
    B. Carson Crosby
    C. Nate Pinkston
    D. Bryson Stewart

48. "The thing I am concerned about…is having something issued so we can convince the public that Oswald is the real assassin."[78]
    A. Hale Boggs
    B. Allen Dulles
    C. Richard Helms
    D. J. Edgar Hoover

49. "We believe there is a conspiracy, no matter how sophisticated or subtle it may be…"[79]
    A. Melvin Belli
    B. F. Lee Bailey
    C. Willie Brandt
    D. Harold Macmillan

50. "Hey Mr. President! Look over here!"[80]
    A. Jean Hill
    B. Karen Day
    C. Mary Miller
    D. Rose Johnson

51. "Sir, when I saw him [Ruby], he was approaching the detectives. It was my first glimpse of it. I personally could not say where he moved from. He came out of the crowd…"[81]
    A. Don Ray Archer
    B. Terence Wallace
    C. Endicott Bellows
    D. Bobby Joe Emerson

52. "Let's get out of here! We are hit!"[82]
    A. Sam Kinney
    B. George Hickey
    C. Emory Roberts
    D. Roy Kellerman

53. "Should I leave well enough alone and disregard the apparent possibility
    that the men who planned the terrible murder are among us today? Should
    I say that the death of Jack Kennedy is not my affair?"[83]
    A. Hale Boggs
    B. Gerald Ford
    C. Jim Garrison
    D. Richard Russell

54. "I was in the motorcade. I was in the White House Press Bus No. 2…I
    heard the last two shots. I didn't know there were three shots until
    sometime later…We tried to get off the bus to see what had happened,
    but we were not allowed to, and the bus went at a high rate of speed out to
    the Dallas Trade Mart."[84]
    A. Hugh Sidey
    B. Seth Kantor
    C. Tom Wicker
    D. Robert Young

55. "When I first heard that sound, I looked up toward that building [TSBD]
    because actually it seemed to come from there."[85]
    A. Joe Neuer
    B. Irv Streator
    C. Earle Brown
    D. Max Phillips

56. "The motorcade had already passed by us and turned back to the north on
    Houston Street. And we heard what we thought to be a shot. And there
    seemed to be a pause between the first shot and the second shot and third
    shots—a little longer pause. And we raced across the street there."[86]
    A. Victor Gibbs
    B. George Kobe
    C. James Embry
    D. Eugene Boone

57. "I got off and walked right by President Kennedy's car. I saw the bouquet of flowers and blood on the upholstery. My first thought was this is serious. There was a clear indication that someone had been hit."[87]
    A. Lem Johns
    B. Ken Jenkins
    C. George Hickey
    D. Roy Kellerman

58. "Then I heard the other two shots and I looked up and the Policeman [Tippit] was in, he seemed like he kind of stumbled and fell."[88]
    A. Dick Miles
    B. Louise Mendez
    C. Domingo Benavides
    D. Janine Cunningham

59. "I was just past that overpass…I didn't hear a shot. I had no idea a shot or shots had been fired."[89]
    A. Dan Rather
    B. Morley Safer
    C. Harry Reasoner
    D. Robert Pierpoint

60. "There was a longer pause between the first and second shots than there was between the second and third shots. They were in rather rapid succession. There was no mistaking in my mind after that, that they were shots from a high-powered rifle."[90]
    A. Earle Cabell
    B. Milton Wright
    C. Raymond Roberts
    D. Homer Thornberry

61. "Suddenly there's a crack—a sharp, cracking sound. People think it's a backfire from a motorcycle, or they think it's a balloon popping."[91]
    A. Robert Caro
    B. Alan Brinkley
    C. Nigel Hamilton
    D. Richard Reeves

62. "There was no way for us to take the prisoner from the homicide office to the jail and back without the news media seeing him. I was besieged actually by the press to permit them to see Oswald. They made such remarks as, 'The public has a right to see, to know,' I didn't want them to think that we were mistreating Oswald."[92]
    A. Stavis Ellis
    B. Jesse Curry
    C. George Lumpkin
    D. Patrick Gannaway

63. "I may be wrong—the US Embassy has ordered him [Oswald] to marry this Russian girl. And a few weeks later, May 16, 1961, he is coming home with the Russian girl. And as we know, he does get out of the Soviet Union with the Russian girl, with money loaned to him by the US Embassy. I may be wrong, gentlemen, but two on two in my book makes four."[93]
    A. Robert Oswald
    B. Charles Murret
    C. Marguerite Oswald
    D. Jeanne de Mohrenschildt

64. "My God, they're going to kill us all!"[94]
    A. Clint Hill
    B. John Connally
    C. Roy Kellerman
    D. Jacqueline Kennedy

65. "When the presidential motorcade came by the Texas School Book
Depository, I was standing on the top step on the first floor...I didn't see
Lee [Oswald]..." [95]
A. Danny Arce
B. Travis Milner
C. James Jarman
D. Buell Wesley Frazier

66. "They knew the whole thing was a cover story. The lone assassin, nobody
believes that, but they know it's unwise to say this."[96]
A. Mort Sahl
B. Lenny Bruce
C. George Carlin
D. Richard Pryor

67. "Now these wild people are chargin' Khrushchev killed Kennedy, and
Castro killed Kennedy, and everybody else killed Kennedy."[97]
A. Joe Biden
B. Donald Trump
C. J. Edgar Hoover
D. Lyndon Johnson

68. "I don't think you should interview her [Jacqueline Kennedy], but after all
she was a witness right alongside of her husband when the bullet struck."[98]
A. Earl Warren
B. John J. McCloy
C. Richard Russell
D. John Sherman Cooper

69. "The president's been shot? My goodness, he's right in front of us!"[99]
A. Ron Hall
B. Everett Smith
C. Barry O'Donnell
D. Nelson Crammer

70. "We have not been told the truth about Oswald."[100]
   A. Jimmy Carter
   B. Richard Russell
   C. Lyndon Johnson
   D. Robert Kennedy

71. "This bullet business leaves me confused…That is very unsatisfactory."[101]
   A. Earl Warren
   B. Gerald Ford
   C. Allen Dulles
   D. John J. McCloy

72. "He [Oswald] was up there and I believe someone asked if he wanted to go down. He said, 'You all close the door on the elevator, I will be down,'…I didn't pay too much attention. He said to leave the elevator come down."[102]
   A. Danny Arce
   B. Charles Givens
   C. Jack Dougherty
   D. Bonnie Ray Williams

73. "Well, it was just a small wound and wasn't jagged like most of the exit bullet wounds that I have seen."[103]
   A. Dolores Pike
   B. Evelyn Rimes
   C. Janine McIntyre
   D. Margaret Henchliffe

74. "I didn't notice very much—I was more concerned with the person in the back of the car—the President. He was very pale, he was lying across Mrs. Kennedy's knee and there seemed to be blood everywhere."[104]
   A. Taylor Levy
   B. Kendra Tyson
   C. Diana Bowron
   D. Cynthia Duggan

75. "Mrs. Kennedy was walking beside the stretcher and the roses that she had been given at the airport were lying on top of the President and her hat was also lying on top of the President as he was brought into the emergency room."[105]
    A. Doris Nelson
    B. Virginia Quinn
    C. Marybeth Toliver
    D. Gwen Stankowski

76. "What better way to destabilize the country…Was this a deliberate attempt by Russia?…Was it the Cubans?…Was it a right-wing hate group, a left-wing group?" [106]
    A. Kemp Clark
    B. Robert Shaw
    C. Evan Brewer
    D. Robert Grossman

77. "Then I was standing here, and as the motorcade turned the corner, I was facing, looking dead at the building. And so, I see this pipe thing sticking out the window. I wasn't paying too much attention to it. Then when the first shot was fired, I started looking around, thinking it was a backfire. Everybody else started looking around. Then I looked up at the window, and he shot again."[107]
    A. Martha Day
    B. Amos Euins
    C. Mindy Davis
    D. James Weaver

78. "Oswald just answered the questions as asked to him. He didn't volunteer any information. He sat there quite stoically, not much of an expression on his face."[108]
    A. Will Fritz
    B. Forrest Sorrels
    C. Winston Lawson
    D. Mitchell DeVinney

79. "Boom, Click-Click, Boom, Click-Click, Boom, Click-Click."[109]
    A. Robin Miller
    B. James Jarman
    C. Harold Norman
    D. Bonnie Ray Williams

80. "It is not surprising that many Americans raised doubts about the Warren Commission...It was heavy with powerful, influential men who rushed through the process and failed to investigate some of the most controversial elements of the case."[110]
    A. Robert Caro
    B. Alan Brinkley
    C. Max Holland
    D. Anthony Summers

81. "President Kennedy grabbed his—looked like he grabbed his ear and blood kept gushing out."[111]
    A. Bill Newman
    B. Mary Redford
    C. Gayle Newman
    D. Abraham Zapruder

82. "I had dealt with death on a daily basis, but here was a president, very much in the prime of his life, killed on a sunny day, in a public place, with scores of people and Secret Service agents around. I had the sudden realization that no one is ever really completely safe, and no one is immortal."[112]
    A. Henry Lee
    B. Cyril Wecht
    C. Michael Baden
    D. Thomas Noguchi

83. "Mr. Johnson, the President is dead."[113]
   A. Lem Johns
   B. Jerry Kivett
   C. Emory Roberts
   D. Mugsy O'Leary

84. "Getting out of the hospital into the cars was one of the swiftest walks I ever made."[114]
   A. Lyndon Johnson
   B. Ralph Yarborough
   C. Lady Bird Johnson
   D. Jacqueline Kennedy

85. "Was it a bomb? A bullet? A firecracker exploding in front of someone's face? And who was hurt?"[115]
   A. J. Edgar Hoover
   B. Robert Kennedy
   C. Hubert Humphrey
   D. Ralph Yarborough

86. "I went to law school after Clay [Shaw] was acquitted to save the world from the likes of Jim Garrison."[116]
   A. Beth Panzeca
   B. Cynthia Wegmann
   C. Michelle Langsford
   D. Rosemarie Dymond

87. "On what basis is it claimed that two shots caused all the wounds?... It seemed to me that Governor Connally's statement negates such a conclusion. I could not agree with this statement."[117]
   A. Robert Dallek
   B. David R. Wrone
   C. Fredrik Logevall
   D. Michael Beschloss

88. "All the cars on the street stopped and pulled over to the side while people cried."[118]
   A. Jane Fonda
   B. Shirley Jones
   C. Tuesday Weld
   D. Audrey Hepburn

89. "You have to stay with it. You just don't pick up a rifle or a pistol or whatever weapon you are using and stay proficient with it. You have to know what you are doing. You have to be a conniver. This boy [Oswald] could have connived the deal, but I think he is a patsy. Somebody else pulled the trigger.[119]
   A. Dean Andrews
   B. Andrew Webber
   C. Evan Constantine
   D. Josiah Zimmerman

90. "I hollered up there to see if he [Lee Bowers] had seen anybody running out there in the freight yards or heard any shots. And he said he didn't hear any shots, and he hadn't seen anybody racing around out there in the yard."[120]
   A. Bryan Little
   B. Harold Travis
   C. Eugene Boone
   D. James Lee Smith

91. "He [Oswald] certainly didn't impress me as anyone capable or anyone burdened with a charge of assassinating the President of the United States, let alone any individual, for that matter. Our conversations were purely the gun magazines, the firearms themselves, and little of anything else."[121]
   A. Cecil Young
   B. Adrian Alba
   C. Seth Wilson
   D. Arthur Rickerby

92. "After the shooting, one of the Secret Service men sitting down in the car in front of us pulled out an automatic rifle or weapon and looked backward. However, all of the Secret Service men seemed to me to respond very slowly, with no more than a puzzled look. In fact, until the automatic weapon was uncovered, I had been lulled into a sense of false hope for the President's safety, by the lack of motion, excitement, or apparent visible knowledge by the Secret Service men, that anything so dreadful was happening..." [122]
   A. Jim Wright
   B. Walter Rogers
   C. George Mahon
   D. Ralph Yarborough

93. "That was one of the only humorous things about the whole thing—somebody did get ahold of the wrong arm, and they were twisting it behind Oswald's back and somebody yelled—I remember that 'My God, you got mine.' I think it was just an arm that come up out of the crowd that somebody grabbed." [123]
   A. Bill Howard
   B. R. D. Stringer
   C. W. R. Westbrook
   D. Robert Ferguson

94. "As we were beginning to go down this incline, all of a sudden there was an explosive noise. I quickly observed unnatural movement of crowds, like ducking or scattering, and quick movements in the Presidential follow-up car. So I turned around and hit the Vice President on the shoulder and hollered, get down, and then looked around again and saw more of this movement, and so I proceeded to go to the back seat and get on top of him." [124]
   A. Henry Rybka
   B. Samuel Sullivan
   C. Rufus Youngblood
   D. William Patterson

95. "By the time the third shot was fired, the car I was in stopped almost through the intersection in front of the Texas School Book Depository Building and I leaped out of the car before the car stopped."[125]
    A. Samuel Kirk
    B. Johnson Smith
    C. Dave Wiegman Jr.
    D. James Underwood

96. "What was that? A firecracker?"[126]
    A. Jack Ready
    B. Paul Landis
    C. Gerald Blaine
    D. Rufus Youngblood

97. "You don't understand me. Kennedy's not going to make it to the election. He is going to be hit."[127]
    A. Carlo Gambino
    B. John Salvatore
    C. Carlos Marcello
    D. Santos Trafficante

98. "I remember being in church on Sunday morning when Lee Harvey Oswald was shot…The church pretty well vacated, and we all ran home to watch the replay of it."[128]
    A. Ed Bradley
    B. Dan Rather
    C. Tom Brokaw
    D. Mike Wallace

99. "My feelings about assassination are identical with Mr. Lincoln's. Anyone who wants to exchange his life for mine can take it."[129]
    A. James Garfield
    B. Ronald Reagan
    C. John F. Kennedy
    D. William McKinley

100. "There is no way of calculating the millions of words that have been uttered in the course of this day, in all countries of this world, as human beings fumble for words to express their offended senses at what has happened in the United States…November the 22nd into the history books, stamped forever with the blackness of this date. I hank you. Good night."[130]
    A. Bill Beutel
    B. Robert Trout
    C. Frank McGee
    D. Mike Wallace

CHAPTER SEVEN ANSWERS

1.   C. Walter Cronkite
2.   B. Walter Cronkite
3.   D. Walter Cronkite
4.   B. Billy Graham
5.   B. Dave Powers
6.   A. Bob Schieffer
7.   C. Buell Wesley Frazier
8.   B. Charles Baxter
9.   B. J. C. Price
10.   D. Hugh Aynesworth
11.   B. Jerry Kivett
12.   B. Emory Roberts
13.   C. Ronald Jones
14.   B. Richard Mosk
15.   C. David A. Kennedy
16.   A. Tina Towner
17.   C. Nicholas Katzenbach
18.   C. Jim Garrison
19.   A. Bobby Hargis
20.   A. Bob Clark
21.   B. Alan Brinkley
22.   B. Albert Bogard
23.   D. Bob Huffaker
24.   A. David Talbot
25.   A. Clint Hill
26.   A. Dean Rusk
27.   D. Michael O'Brien
28.   D. Clyde Haygood
29.   D. Wesley Liebeler
30.   B. Ike Pappas
31.   C. Bob Jackson
32.   C. Bob Huffaker

33. B. Abraham Zapruder
34. A. Jim Garrison
35. A. Liz Carpenter
36. D. Ted Callaway
37. B. Ronald Jones
38. D. Cliff Robertson
39. C. Royce Skelton
40. B. James Jarman
41. D. Lyndon Johnson
42. B. Malcolm Couch
43. A. Tom Dillard
44. B. James Worrell
45. A. Robert Oswald
46. C. James Altgens
47. A. Billy Lovelady
48. D. J. Edgar Hoover
49. A. Melvin Belli
50. A. Jean Hill
51. A. Don Ray Archer
52. D. Roy Kellerman
53. C. Jim Garrison
54. B. Seth Kantor
55. C. Earle Brown
56. D. Eugene Boone
57. A. Lem Johns
58. C. Domingo Benavides
59. A. Dan Rather
60. A. Earle Cabell
61. A. Robert Caro
62. B. Jesse Curry
63. C. Marguerite Oswald
64. B. John Connally
65. D. Buell Wesley Frazier
66. A. Mort Sahl
67. D. Lyndon Johnson

68. B. John J. McCloy
69. A. Ron Hall
70. B. Richard Russell
71. D. John J. McCloy
72. A. Danny Arce
73. D. Margaret Henchliffe
74. C. Diana Bowron
75. A. Doris Nelson
76. D. Robert Grossman
77. B. Amos Euins
78. C. Winston Lawson
79. C. Harold Norman
80. B. Alan Brinkley
81. C. Gayle Newman
82. B. Cyril Wecht
83. C. Emory Roberts
84. C. Lady Bird Johnson
85. D. Ralph Yarborough
86. B. Cynthia Wegmann
87. B. David R. Wrone
88. A. Jane Fonda
89. A. Dean Andrews
90. C. Eugene Boone
91. B. Adrian Alba
92. D. Ralph Yarborough
93. C. W. R. Westbrook
94. C. Rufus Youngblood
95. D. James Underwood
96. A. Jack Ready
97. D. Santos Trafficante
98. C. Tom Brokaw
99. C. John F. Kennedy
100. C. Frank McGee

CHAPTER EIGHT

LITERATURE

1. In *The Ruby-Oswald Affair*, Jack Ruby appears in a photograph with this legendary country music artist.
   A. Buck Owens
   B. Hank Williams
   C. Marty Robbins
   D. Tennessee Ernie Ford

2. Which 1992 publication by Bonar Menninger claimed that a Secret Service agent accidentally fired the fatal shot that killed President Kennedy?
   A. *Mortal Error*
   B. *Reckless Intent*
   C. *Mistaken Identity*
   D. *Flawed Judgement*

3. The title of Don DeLillo's best-selling novel *Libra* was taken from whose astrological sign?
   A. Jack Ruby
   B. Lyndon Johnson
   C. Robert Kennedy
   D. Lee Harvey Oswald

4. Name the only member of the WC to publish a book about the JFK assassination.
   A. Hale Boggs
   B. Gerald Ford
   C. Richard Russell
   D. John Sherman Cooper

5. All of the following were written by US Senate investigator Harold Weisberg *except* _____.
   A. *Whitewash: The Report on the Warren Commission*
   B. *Government Cover-Up: The JFK Assassination Exposed*
   C. *Never Again! The Government Conspiracy in the JFK Assassination*
   D. *Lee Harvey Oswald in New Orleans: Case for Conspiracy with the CIA*

6. Published in French and later translated into English, it was the first critique of the WC and its findings.
   A. *Scapegoat*
   B. *The Oswald Affair*
   C. *Sandbagging History*
   D. *Who was Lee Harvey Oswald?*

7. In this 1980 bestseller, author David Lifton concluded that preautopsy surgery had been performed on the body of JFK.
   A. *Killing JFK*
   B. *Dallas 1963*
   C. *Best Evidence*
   D. *Dallas to Bethesda*

8. What if November 22, 1963, had never happened? That question is the focus of this cleverly written novel by Emmy-winning journalist and political analyst Jeff Greenfield.
   A. *Destiny Fulfilled: An Alternative History of the JFK Presidency*
   B. *A Man for All Seasons: The Two Terms of President John Kennedy*
   C. *Then Nothing Changed: How JFK and America Survived November 1963*
   D. *If Kennedy Lived: The First and Second Terms of President John F. Kennedy*

9. The chief counsel to the HSCA from 1977 to 1978, he later authored *The Plot to Kill the President*.
    A. Terry Lenzner
    B. Samuel Devine
    C. Donald Sanders
    D. None of the above

10. Journalist Jim Bishop provided a minute-by-minute account of JFK's death in _____.
    A. *Dallas Justice*
    B. *High Noon in Texas*
    C. *The Day Kennedy Was Shot*
    D. *Countdown from Love Field*

11. The author of *Assignment Oswald*, he was the FBI agent who surveilled Marina Oswald following her arrival in the US.
    A. James Hosty
    B. Arthur Ward
    C. James Rhodes
    D. Thomas Colby

12. Published in 1980, it was the first scholarly compilation of JFK assassination sources.
    A. *Who's Who in the JFK Assassination*
    B. *A Bibliographic Assessment of the Kennedy Murder*
    C. *November 22, 1963: A Reference Guide to the JFK Assassination*
    D. *The Assassination of John F. Kennedy: A Comprehensive Historical and Legal Bibliography, 1963–1979*

13. In his groundbreaking book *Six Seconds in Dallas*, this Haverford College professor turned private investigator determined that four shooters were involved in the Kennedy assassination.
    A. Jack Moore
    B. Michael Kurtz
    C. Josiah Thompson
    D. Sean Cunningham

14. Of the following titles, which one was the abridged version of Richard B. Trask's *Pictures of the Pain: Photography and the Assassination of President Kennedy*?
    A. *Southern Justice*
    B. *Death of a Prince*
    C. *That Day in Dallas*
    D. *Dallas: November 1963*

15. Name the actor, politician, and professional wrestler who published *They've Killed Our President*.
    A. Jesse Ventura
    B. Randy Savage
    C. Eddie Guerrero
    D. Shawn Michaels

16. Best known for prosecuting Charles Manson for the Tate-LaBianca murders, he was the author of *Reclaiming History: The Assassination of President John F. Kennedy*.
    A. Gil Garcetti
    B. Vincent Bugliosi
    C. Johnny Cochran
    D. Robert Philibosian

17. Which of these books was published on the tenth anniversary of the Kennedy assassination?
    A. *Legacy of Doubt*
    B. *Treachery in Dallas*
    C. *Where Angels Tread Lightly*
    D. *Trauma Room One: The JFK Medical Cover-Up*

18. Known for his sardonic manner on *Law & Order: SVU*, he penned the 2013 *Hit List: An In-Depth Investigation into the Mysterious Deaths of Witnesses to the JFK Assassination.*
    A. Iced-T
    B. Dann Florek
    C. Richard Belzer
    D. Christopher Meloni

19. Written by Jerome R. Corsi, it implicated organized crime, Richard Nixon, and the French in Kennedy's murder.
    A. *Sorrow in Autumn*
    B. *Kennedy's Never Cry*
    C. *Triumvirate of Death*
    D. *Who Really Killed Kennedy?*

20. For his book, *The Death of a President*, William Manchester was granted exclusive access to all of the following *except* _____.
    A. Earl Warren
    B. Marina Oswald
    C. Lady Bird Johnson
    D. Jacqueline Kennedy

21. Which group allegedly contracted three Corsican hitmen to kill JFK in Steven J. Rivele's *The Murderers of John F. Kennedy?*
    A. CIA
    B. NSC
    C. KGB
    D. Mafia

22. In the February 1995 issue of *The Journal of Southern History*, author and historian David R. Wrone said that "Massive numbers of factual errors suffuse the book, which make it a veritable minefield." Which publication was Wrone referring to?[131]
    A. *Death Wish*
    B. *Case Closed*
    C. *Reclaiming History*
    D. None of the above

23. Name the conspiracy theorist and author who ran with comedian Dick Gregory as write-in candidates for president in 1968.
    A. Mark Lane
    B. Cyril Wecht
    C. Richard Popkin
    D. Anthony Summers

24. In James Ellroy's novel *American Tabloid*, the main characters conspire to assassinate JFK during a _____ motorcade.
    A. Miami
    B. Denver
    C. Boston
    D. Portland

25. *Case Open* was a repudiation of this pro-Warren Commission bestseller.
    A. *Case Closed*
    B. *The Warren Commission Was Correct*
    C. *Conclusive: Oswald and the Crime of the Century*
    D. *The Scavengers and Critics of the Warren Report*

26. In his 2012 book _____, author Peter Janney explored the connection between Mary Pinchot Meyer and JFK, the assassination in Dallas, and her unsolved murder.

    A *Mary's Diary*

    B. *Mary's Secret*

    C. *Mary's Mosaic*

    D. *Mary's Murder*

27. Which member of Oswald's family wrote *Lee: A Portrait of Lee Harvey Oswald*?

    A. June Oswald

    B. Robert Oswald

    C. Marina Oswald

    D. Audrey Oswald

28. A photo-optics technician turned assassination researcher, he served as a photographic consultant for the HSCA and later as an adviser on the film *JFK*. His best-known works include *The Search for Lee Harvey Oswald: A Comprehensive Photographic Record* and *The Killing of a President: The Complete Photographic Record of the JFK Assassination, the Conspiracy, and the Cover-Up*.

    A. Jerry Mueller

    B. F. Peter Model

    C. Robert Groden

    D. Harrison Livingston

29. She was a former World Health Organization official who published a comprehensive index of the Warren Commission's report.

    A. Mary Ferrell

    B. Abby Mitchum

    C. Sylvia Meagher

    D. Eugenie Cheyney

30. Who wrote the novel *November 22, 1963*?
    A. Jay Ely
    B. Adam Braver
    C. James Fletcher
    D. Charlotte Watkins

31. The author of *Who Killed JFK?* and *The JFK Assassination: The Facts and Theories*, he was the cofounder of the Boston-based Assassination Information Bureau.
    A. Todd Gitlin
    B. Jerry Rubin
    C. Tom Hayden
    D. Carl Oglesby

32. In *Legend: The Secret World of Lee Harvey Oswald*, there is a photograph of Lee Harvey Oswald and which Hollywood icon?
    A. Clark Gable
    B. John Wayne
    C. Rock Hudson
    D. James Stewart

33. Bill O'Reilly wrote the book and Rob Lowe starred in the TV-movie that came from the book.
    A. *Red Roses in Texas*
    B. *The Dream Died in Dallas*
    C. *Code Name Lancer: The JFK Assassination*
    D. None of the above

34. An anti-Castro Cuban who debated Lee Harvey Oswald on a New Orleans radio show, he authored *Red Friday: November 22, 1963*.
    A. Oscar Tomayo
    B. Manuel Ortega
    C. Hiram Martinez
    D. Carlos Bringuier

35. In *Deadly Secrets*, journalist Warren Hinckle examined the undeclared war between the US government and Cuba and a possible CIA plot to assassinate JFK. What was the book's original title?
    A. *The Fish Is Red*
    B. *Night of the Iguana*
    C. *The Sons of San Cristobal*
    D. *If You Have a Lemon, Make Lemonade*

36. The late author and literary critic Donald Graham said, "When anybody asks me what Dallas was like during the time of the Kennedy assassination, I always refer them to one book." Which was he referencing?[132]
    A. *Winter Soldier*
    B. *Strange Peaches*
    C. *Night Never Falls*
    D. *Forbidden Dangers*

37. Apart from writing *Plausible Denial* and *Last Word*, he founded the Citizens' Committee of Inquiry.
    A. Mark Lane
    B. Leo Sauvage
    C. John Armstrong
    D. Vincent J. Salandria

38. Published in 2002 by historical novelist Thomas Mallon, it concluded that Ruth Paine was an innocent victim of the Kennedy assassination.
    A. *Collateral Damage*
    B. *Mrs. Paine's Garage*
    C. *Innocent of Involvement*
    D. *Mrs. Paine's Conundrum*

39. Name the long-awaited 2021 sequel to *Six Seconds in Dallas*.
    A. *Last Second in Dallas*
    B. *Twenty-Seven Hours in Texas*
    C. *Fourteen Seconds in Dealey Plaza*
    D. *Six Seconds in the Life of President Kennedy*

40. Originally titled *L'Amerique Brule*, it linked corporate and intelligence interests to Kennedy's murder.
   A. *Deadly Cabal*
   B. *Farewell America:The Plot to Kill JFK*
   C. *JFK:Why the President's Death Matters*
   D. *How the Private and Public Sector Murdered Kennedy*

41. A former Los Angeles homicide detective, who played a controversial role in the O.J. Simpson investigation, he would later go on to write several books including *A Simple Act of Murder: November 22, 1963*.
   A. Tom Lange
   B. Peter Malloy
   C. Mark Fuhrman
   D. Philip Vannatter

42. Oliver Stone called this book by Catholic theologian and peace activist James W. Douglass, "The best account I have read of this tragedy and its significance."[133]
   A. *Please Forgive My Grief*
   B. *JFK: Murder and Redemption*
   C. *Murder on the 22nd of November*
   D. *JFK and the Unspeakable:Why He Died andWhy It Matters*

43. In which 1974 novel did a US intelligence officer suspect that the South Vietnamese assassinated JFK in retaliation for the murder of Ngo Dinh Diem?
   A. *The Raven Calls*
   B. *Deadly Revenge*
   C. *The Tears of Autumn*
   D. *Voices from Lampang*

44. "Even if it was cloudy or raining that day, the country and world were more innocent and optimistic at that moment than they have been since then." This is a quote from _____. [134]
   A. *On An Autumn Day in Dealey Plaza*
   B. *JFK: An Attempt to Make Sense of the Tragic Events in Dallas*
   C. *Death of the Rising Sun: A Search for Truth in the John F. Kennedy Assassination*
   D. *Making Sense of the Tragic Death of President John F. Kennedy in the Lone Star State*

45. The author of *Marina and Lee*, she was the only journalist who knew both John F. Kennedy and Lee Harvey Oswald.
   A. Lara Logan
   B. Denise Curry
   C. Barbara Tuchman
   D. Priscilla Johnson McMillan

46. A member of JFK's security detail, his experiences on that fateful weekend were recounted in the best-selling memoir *Five Days in November*.
   A. Clint Hill
   B. James Sloan
   C. Roy Kellerman
   D. Winston Lawson

47. In which of the following books did Craig I. Zirbel link Vice President Lyndon Johnson to the Kennedy assassination?
   A. *Justice Texas Style*
   B. *The Texas Connection*
   C. *High Noon in Dealey Plaza*
   D. *Lyndon B. Johnson: Blind Ambition*

48. The coauthor of *JFK: The Last Dissenting Witness*, she was dubbed the "Lady in Red" because of the distinctive red raincoat she wore in Dealey Plaza.
   A. Jean Hill
   B. Mary Moorman
   C. Daphne Watkins
   D. Marilyn Sitzman

49. An investigative journalist who reportedly witnessed the assassination of JFK, and Lee Harvey Oswald's arrest and subsequent murder, he is the author of *November 22, 1963: Witness to History.*
    A. Dan Rather
    B. James Ewell
    C. Robert MacNeil
    D. Hugh Aynesworth

50. Which book was reissued as *Four Days in November: The Assassination of President John F. Kennedy?*
    A. *Reclaiming History*
    B. *A Case of Conspiracy*
    C. *Presumption of Guilt*
    D. *Reasonable Suspicion*

51. In this 2018 bestseller by Lou Berney, a Mafia lieutenant running from his past, and a housewife running from her husband, meet on the open road in the days following the JFK assassination.
    A. *November Road*
    B. *Dangerous Liaison*
    C. *Highway to the Future*
    D. *Strangers When We Meet*

52. Which was nominated for the Pulitzer Prize in History?
    A. *Case Closed*
    B. *Best Evidence*
    C. *Executive Action*
    D. *Heritage of Stone*

53. This was Warren Commission critic Edward Jay Epstein's first book on the JFK assassination.
    A. *Counterplot*
    B. *Legend: The Secret World of Lee Harvey Oswald*
    C. *Inquest: The Warren Commission and the Establishment of Truth*
    D. *The JFK Assassination Diary: My Search for Answers to the Mystery of the Century*

54. An award-winning journalist and author of *Top Down: A Novel of the Kennedy Assassination*, he was also the executive editor and anchor of the *PBS NewsHour*.
    A. Jim Lehrer
    B. Ray Suarez
    C. David Brinkley
    D. John Chancellor

55. The first African American assigned to a presidential security detail, he accused the Secret Service of badly mishandling JFK's protection in Dallas in his memoir *The Echo from Dealey Plaza*. Convicted of bribery charges in 1964, he was pardoned by President Joe Biden in 2022.
    A. William Miller
    B. Charles Gittens
    C. Abraham Bolden
    D. Clarence Washington

56. Name the doctor who erroneously claimed in his 1992 book *JFK: Conspiracy of Silence* that preautopsy surgery had been performed on President Kennedy.
    A. Malcolm Perry
    B. Charles Carrico
    C. Adolph Giesecke
    D. Charles Crenshaw

57. A witness to the JFK assassination, he was the author of *Truth Withheld: A Survivor's Story* and *LBJ and the Kennedy Killing*.
    A. Lee Bowers
    B. James Tague
    C. Billy Lovelady
    D. Gordon Arnold

58. "When John F. Kennedy entered the presidential limousine at Love
    Field, he began his ride into history. The journey continues. We call it the
    Kennedy legacy." This quote is from which Larry J. Sabato book?[135]
    A. *When Powers Collide*
    B. *The Kennedy Half-Century*
    C. *President Kennedy: Profile of Power*
    D. *The JFK Legacy: From Boston to Arlington*

59. A Harvard lawyer and researcher, he founded the Committee to
    Investigate Assassinations and the Washington-based Assassination
    Archives and Research Center. In 1977 he published *Assassination of JFK: By
    Coincidence or Conspiracy?*
    A. James Lesar
    B. Larry Howard
    C. George Russell
    D. Bernard Fensterwald Jr.

60. Written by John H. Davis, *Mafia Kingfish* linked the Kennedy assassination
    to which organized crime figure?
    A. Paul Castellano
    B. Carlos Marcello
    C. Joseph Columbo
    D. Carmine Galante

61. A former assistant district attorney and deputy chief counsel to the HSCA,
    he authored the 1994 *New York Times* bestseller *Corruption of Blood*.
    A. G. Robert Blakey
    B. Richard A. Sprague
    C. Thomas N. Downing
    D. Robert K. Tanenbaum

62. Of these books, which was released on the twenty-fifth anniversary of Kennedy's death?
   A. *Not in Your Lifetime*
   B. *The Ruby-Oswald Affair*
   C. *Why Did You Kill Your President?*
   D. *The Truth about the JFK Assassination*

63. Known as the "Babushka Lady," Beverly Oliver claimed that prior to November 22, 1963, she was introduced to Lee Harvey Oswald by Jack Ruby. In 1994, she penned an assassination memoir entitled _____.
   A. *Nightmare in Dallas*
   B. *Death in Dealey Plaza*
   C. *Nightmare on Elm Street*
   D. *I Was the Babushka Lady*

64. A distinguished urologist, military collector, and author of *Kennedy and Lincoln: Medical and Ballistic Comparisons of Their Assassinations*, he was selected by the Kennedy family in 1972 to examine JFK's autopsy photographs and X-rays. He later concluded that there was a high probability Lee Harvey Oswald had fired the shots that killed Kennedy.
   A. Cyril H. Wecht
   B. John K. Lattimer
   C. Michael M. Baden
   D. Thomas T. Noguchi

65. Written by Steven M. Gillon, it detailed the challenges faced by President Lyndon Johnson in the hours following JFK's death. It was also the basis for the 2009 History Channel documentary of the same name.
   A. *The JFK Assassination: Minute by Minute*
   B. *Lyndon Baines Johnson: President in Crisis*
   C. *The Kennedy Assassination: 24 Hours Later*
   D. *November 22, 1963: The Dallas to Washington Timeline*

66. Published in 1991, *Act of Treason* accused _____ of concealing evidence of a Mafia plot to murder President Kennedy.
    A. Dean Rusk
    B. Richard Nixon
    C. J. Edgar Hoover
    D. Robert Kennedy

67. A lawyer and author of *The Oswald Files*, he claimed that a Russian look-alike, not Lee Harvey Oswald, killed Kennedy.
    A. Peter Dale Scott
    B. Joachim Joesten
    C. Michael Eddowes
    D. Fletcher Marlboro

68. Which of the following titles point to CIA involvement in the death of JFK?
    A. *First Hand Knowledge*
    B. *The Building on Elm Street*
    C. *Assassination: Inside the Agency*
    D. *JFK: The Greatest Possible Conspiracy*

69. In 2013, this Trump devotee and conspiracy wonk authored *The Man Who Killed Kennedy*.
    A. Roger Stone
    B. Rudy Giuliani
    C. Steve Bannon
    D. Paul Manafort

70. This book by JFK researcher and photographic consultant to the HSCA, Richard E. Sprague, was discovered on the bookshelf of Osama Bin Laden following his death.
    A. *The Conspiracy of One*
    B. *Downfall of the President*
    C. *The Taking of America, 1-2-3*
    D. *Subterfuge and Assassination*

71. Name the Dallas Police officer who was a witness at the Clay Shaw trial and was also the author of *When They Kill a President*.
    A. Glen King
    B. Roger Craig
    C. Neal Talbot
    D. Richard Cox

72. Based on extensive research, this book by Lamar Waldron concluded that the murder of JFK by Carlos Marcello and Santos Trafficante was designed to secure the survival of the Mafia.
    A. *The Italian Connection*
    B. *Dallas Hit: Jack, Santos, and Carlos*
    C. *The Hidden History of the JFK Assassination*
    D. *Assassination in Dallas: The Ultimate Contract*

73. Publicized as an "objective" study of conspiracies, it dealt more with the sexual behavior of JFK, Marilyn Monroe, and J. Edgar Hoover.
    A. *History Unraveled*
    B. *Conspiracy in Camelot*
    C. *Liaison: JFK and Monroe*
    D. *The Assassination Game*

74. Written by Michael Canfield and Alan J. Weberman, it contended that Watergate participants E. Howard Hunt and Frank Sturgis were involved in the Dallas shooting.
    A. *Coup in America*
    B. *JFK: Coup in Dallas*
    C. *Executive Coup d'Etat*
    D. *Coup d'Etat in America*

75. A veteran journalist and researcher for the HSCA, he was the author of *The Last Investigation*.
    A. Gaeton Fonzi
    B. Eric Konigsberg
    C. Michael Callahan
    D. Christopher McDougall

76. Considered the last word on the murder of Dallas Police officer J. D. Tippit, it was written by Emmy-winning animator and JFK assassinologist Dale K. Myers.
    A. *With Malice*
    B. *An Ironclad Case*
    C. *Murder in Oak Cliff*
    D. *Oswald Killed Tippit*

77. Released in 2012 by former US intelligence specialist Brian Latell, this book claimed that Fidel Castro had foreknowledge of the Kennedy assassination.
    A. *Duplicity: The JFK Assassination*
    B. *Castro and the Plot to Kill Kennedy*
    C. *Vendetta! Fidel Castro and the Kennedy Brothers*
    D. *Castro's Secrets: The CIA and Cuba's Intelligence Machine*

78. A former NBC News correspondent and author of *The Way We Were: 1963: The Year Kennedy Was Shot*, he *may* have encountered Lee Harvey Oswald in the doorway of the TSBD moments after the shooting.
    A. Elie Abel
    B. Morley Safer
    C. Peter Jennings
    D. Robert MacNeil

79. Who was the Russian professor who chronicled his relationship with Lee Harvey Oswald in *Lee Harvey Oswald: As I Knew Him*?
    A. Dimitry Turgenev
    B. Sergey Preobrazhensky
    C. George de Mohrenschildt
    D. Alexander Chernyshevsky

80. All of the following books were published on the thirtieth anniversary of the JFK assassination *except* _____.
    A. *How Kennedy Was Killed?*
    B. *Deep State Politics and the Death of Camelot*
    C. *The Mafia Plot to Assassinate President John Kennedy*
    D. None of the above

81. In *Breach of Faith: How the Warren Commission Failed the Nation and Why*, author Gerald D. McKnight concluded that powerful forces in the US government had predetermined that any investigation must conclude that _____.
    A. Lee Harvey Oswald was a patsy
    B. Jack Ruby was not the second gunman
    C. Vice President Johnson was not involved
    D. Lee Harvey Oswald was the lone assassin

82. Released three years after the Clay Shaw trial, it was Jim Garrison's first book about JFK's murder.
    A. *Unequal Justice*
    B. *Heritage of Stone*
    C. *Goodbye to Justice*
    D. *The Star Spangled Contract*

83. In _____, political activist and author Carl Oglesby argued that a shift in America's power structure was responsible for the death of President Kennedy and the downfall of Richard Nixon.
    A. *The Cold and Hot War*
    B. *The Blue and Gray War*
    C. *The Yankee and Cowboy War*
    D. *The Good Guy and Bad Guy War*

84. Using declassified documents under the JFK Assassination Records Act, this former US Army officer linked Lee Harvey Oswald to US intelligence in *Oswald and the CIA*.
    A. Tom Clancy
    B. Paul Fussell
    C. John Newman
    D. David Hackworth

85. The former medical examiner of San Antonio, Texas, Dr. Vincent Di Maio called it, "the only book to address the firearms and ballistic aspects of the JFK assassination in a logical, knowledgeable, and scientific manner."[136]
    A. *Case Solved: Falsehoods and Misconceptions in the Death of JFK*
    B. *The JFK Myths: A Scientific Investigation of the Kennedy Assassination*
    C. *Expert Witness: Assassination Science and the Murder of John F. Kennedy*
    D. *Logic and the JFK Murder: A Minute-by-Minute Study of the Crime of the Century*

86. In this collection of essays by Dean R. Owens, the famous and not-so-famous shared their thoughts on the life and tragic death of President John F. Kennedy.
    A. *JFK: In Their Own Words*
    B. *A Remembrance of Jack*
    C. *How We Remember Him*
    D. *November 22, 1963: Reflections on the Life, Assassination, and Legacy of John F. Kennedy*

87. The last surviving passenger in the JFK limousine, Nellie Connally recounted her experiences in _____.
    A. *From Love Field*
    B. *Texas Welcomes You*
    C. *Welcome Mr. President*
    D. *Red Roses for Mrs. Kennedy*

88. Which of the following books was not written by longtime assassination critic and scholar Peter Dale Scott?
    A. *Oswald, Mexico, and Deep Politics*
    B. *Southern Cabal: Kennedy in Dallas*
    C. *Deep Politics and the Death of JFK*
    D. *The Assassination: Dallas and Beyond*

89. Originally released in France, under the title *L'Amerique Brute*, it described a variety of forces that conspired against the Kennedy brothers.
    A. *Farewell America*
    B. *America Is Watching*
    C. *The Burning of America*
    D. *American Horror Story*

90. Written by the former chief of Cuban counterintelligence, Fabian Escalante, *JFK: The Cuban Files* implicated all the following groups in a conspiracy to murder JFK *except* the _____.
    A. CIA
    B. KGB
    C. Mafia
    D. Cuban exiles

91. In this 1986 novel by Stanley Shapiro, David Russell travels back in time to alter the events in Dallas to save his brother who was killed in the Vietnam War.
    A. *Instant Replay*
    B. *A Time to Remember*
    C. *The 22nd of November*
    D. *Sherlock Holmes in Dallas*

92. Which veteran newspaper reporter and acquaintance of Jack Ruby wrote *The Ruby Cover-Up*?
    A. Seth Kantor
    B. Tom Wicker
    C. Bob Schieffer
    D. Gerald Huffington

93. A former US Air Force officer and the inspiration for the "Mr. X" character in the film *JFK*, he was the author of *JFK: The CIA, Vietnam, and the Plot to Assassinate Kennedy*.
    A. Charles Rich
    B. Fletcher Prouty
    C. Lawrence Benjamin
    D. Gerald Breckenridge

94. In *A Cruel and Shocking Act: The Secret History of the Kennedy Assassination*, Philip Shenon tells the story of how the _____ was unable or unwilling to uncover the truth surrounding the death of President Kennedy.
    A. WC
    B. CIA
    C. FBI
    D. NSA

95. How the media defined the events in Dallas and shaped our impressions beyond the tragedy were examined in this 1992 book by former journalist and University of Pennsylvania professor Barbie Zelizer.
    A. *Covering the Body*
    B. *The News Vacuum*
    C. *All the News That's Fit to Print*
    D. *Flash: The President's Been Shot*

96. Of the following books, which was released on the fiftieth anniversary of the JFK assassination?
   A. *The Garrison Case*
   B. *JFK: The Second Plot*
   C. *The Zapruder Film Hoax*
   D. None of the above

97. Name the syndicated columnist whose sudden death and connection to Jack Ruby was the subject of Mark Shaw's *Denial of Justice*.
   A. Jack Anderson
   B. Louella Parsons
   C. Nigel Dempster
   D. Dorothy Kilgallen

98. An award-winning journalist, editor, and consultant for National Geographic Television, he authored *The Kennedy Assassination Tapes: The White House Conversations of Lyndon B. Johnson regarding the Assassination, the Warren Commission, and the Aftermath.*
   A. Roger Adair
   B. Max Holland
   C. Frank Camper
   D. Ralph Thomas

99. The *Library Journal* called it a significant addition to JFK research because "it presents in riveting detail the assassination from the agents' perspective." Which book by Gerald Blaine and Lisa McCubbin received this review?[137]
   A. *The Kennedy Detail*
   B. *Five Days in November*
   C. *Guarding John F. Kennedy*
   D. *20 Years in the Secret Service*

100. A trained psychiatric nurse, her study of JFK's alleged assassin was the basis for *The Mind of Oswald* and *Autobiography of Lee Harvey Oswald*.
A. Linda Mauer
B. Diane Holloway
C. Valarie Grunberg
D. Brianna Kellmare

CHAPTER EIGHT ANSWERS

1. D. Tennessee Ernie Ford
2. A. *Mortal Error*
3. D. Lee Harvey Oswald
4. B. Gerald Ford
5. B. *Government Cover-Up: The JFK Assassination Exposed*
6. B. *The Oswald Affair*
7. C. *Best Evidence*
8. D. *If Kennedy Lived: The First and Second Terms of President John F. Kennedy*
9. D. None of the above
10. C. *The Day Kennedy Was Shot*
11. A. James Hosty
12. D. *The Assassination of John F. Kennedy: A Comprehensive Historical and Legal Bibliography, 1963–1979*
13. C. Josiah Thompson
14. C. *That Day in Dallas*
15. A. Jesse Ventura
16. B. Vincent Bugliosi
17. A. *Legacy of Doubt*
18. C. Richard Belzer
19. D. *Who Really Killed Kennedy?*
20. B. Marina Oswald
21. D. Mafia
22. B. *Case Closed*
23. A. Mark Lane
24. A. Miami
25. A. *Case Closed*
26. C. *Mary's Mosaic*
27. B. Robert Oswald
28. C. Robert Groden
29. C. Sylvia Meagher
30. B. Adam Braver

31. D. Carl Oglesby
32. B. John Wayne
33. D. None of the above
34. D. Carlos Bringuier
35. A. *The Fish Is Red*
36. B. *Strange Peaches*
37. A. Mark Lane
38. B. *Mrs. Paine's Garage*
39. A. *Last Second in Dallas*
40. B. *Farewell America: The Plot to Kill JFK*
41. C. Mark Fuhrman
42. D. *JFK and the Unspeakable: Why He Died and Why It Matters*
43. C. *The Tears of Autumn*
44. C. *Death of the Rising Son: A Search for Truth in the John F. Kennedy Assassination*
45. D. Priscilla Johnson McMillan
46. A. Clint Hill
47. B. *The Texas Connection*
48. A. Jean Hill
49. D. Hugh Aynesworth
50. A. *Reclaiming History*
51. A. *November Road*
52. A. *Case Closed*
53. C. *Inquest: The Warren Commission and the Establishment of Truth*
54. A. Jim Lehrer
55. C. Abraham Bolden
56. D. Charles Crenshaw
57. B. James Tague
58. B. *The Kennedy Half-Century*
59. D. Bernard Fensterwald Jr.
60. B. Carlos Marcello
61. D. Robert K. Tanenbaum
62. B. *The Ruby-Oswald Affair*
63. A. *Nightmare in Dallas*

64. B. John K. Lattimer
65. C. *The Kennedy Assassination: 24 Hours Later*
66. C. J. Edgar Hoover
67. C. Michael Eddowes
68. A. *First Hand Knowledge*
69. A. Roger Stone
70. C. *The Taking of America, 1-2-3*
71. B. Roger Craig
72. C. *The Hidden History of the JFK Assassination*
73. B. *Conspiracy in Camelot*
74. D. *Coup d'Etat in America*
75. A. Gaeton Fonzi
76. A. *With Malice*
77. D. *Castro's Secrets: The CIA and Cuba's Intelligence Machine*
78. D. Robert MacNeil
79. C. George de Mohrenschildt
80. D. None of the above
81. D. Lee Harvey Oswald was the lone assassin
82. B. *Heritage of Stone*
83. C. *The Yankee and Cowboy War*
84. C. John Newman
85. B. *The JFK Myths: A Scientific Investigation of the Kennedy Assassination*
86. D. *November 22, 1963: Reflections on the Life, Assassination, and Legacy of John F. Kennedy*
87. A. *From Love Field*
88. B. *Southern Cabal: Kennedy in Dallas*
89. A. *Farewell America*
90. B. KGB
91. B. *A Time to Remember*
92. A. Seth Kantor
93. B. Fletcher Prouty
94. A. WC
95. A. *Covering the Body*

96. D. None of the above
97. D. Dorothy Kilgallen
98. B. Max Holland
99. A. *The Kennedy Detail*
100. B. Diane Holloway

CHAPTER NINE

DOCUMENTARIES, FILMS, AND TV PROGRAMS

1. Branded a Communist sympathizer in the late 1940s, he later went on to write the screenplay for such films as *Spartacus* and *Executive Action*, a fictionalized account of the Kennedy assassination.
   A. Dalton Trumbo
   B. Martin Scorsese
   C. William Goldman
   D. Francis Ford Coppola

2. Which outspoken critics of the WC made cameo appearances in Oliver Stone's *JFK?*
   A. Cyril Wecht and Gerald Posner
   B. Jim Garrison and Robert Groden
   C. Mark Lane and Josiah Thompson
   D. Jerry Policoff and Anthony Summers

3. The tagline for this documentary was, "On November 22, 1963, John F. Kennedy was murdered, and the truth was buried."[138]
   A. *Contract on America*
   B. *The JFK Investigation*
   C. *Rendezvous in Dallas: The Oswald Files*
   D. *The JFK Assassination: The Jim Garrison Tapes*

4. Who portrayed JFK in the 2011 TV miniseries *The Kennedys*?
   A. Barry Pepper
   B. Greg Kinnear
   C. Giovanni Ribisi
   D. Stephen Roach

5. According to author John Loken, Lee Harvey Oswald was influenced by the following films *except* _____.
   A. *Psycho*
   B. *Suddenly*
   C. *We Were Strangers*
   D. *The Manchurian Candidate*

6. Name the Rhodes scholar, actor, and member of the musical group The Highwaymen who played a Texas Border Patrol officer in the JFK assassination thriller *Flashpoint*.
   A. Willie Nelson
   B. George Strait
   C. Waylon Jennings
   D. Kris Kristofferson

7. In which film did the protagonist say, "I was in Dallas on November 22, 1963. That mean anything to you?"[139]
   A. *The Contract Killer*
   B. *Presidential Sanction*
   C. *Interview with the Assassin*
   D. *The November Conspirators*

8. Who was the actor that portrayed Lee Harvey Oswald in *Fatal Deception: Mrs. Lee Harvey Oswald* and an Oswald imposter in *JFK*?
   A. Ron Eldard
   B. Gary Sinese
   C. Ethan Hawke
   D. Frank Whaley

9. Best known for his comedic work on *Rowan and Martin's Laugh-In*,
    he costarred as Dallas Police Chief Jesse Curry in the 2003 film *The
    Commission.*
    A. Larry Hovis
    B. Arte Johnson
    C. Henry Gibson
    D. Richard Dawson

10. Which line of dialogue in *The Irishman* hints at mob involvement in JFK's
    assassination?[140]
    A. "Well, I guess Hoffa got what he wanted."
    B. "They whacked the wrong Kennedy brother."
    C. "His father's money couldn't protect him this time."
    D. "If they can knock off a president, they can knock off the president of a
    union."

11. In *Jackie*, who was originally cast to play Jacqueline Kennedy?
    A. Diane Lane
    B. Rachel Weisz
    C. Keira Knightley
    D. Natalie Portman

12. Of the following actors, which were offered the role of Jim Garrison in
    JFK, but respectfully declined?
    A. Tom Hanks and John Travolta
    B. Mel Gibson and Harrison Ford
    C. Ben Affleck and George Clooney
    D. Robert De Niro and Jack Nicholson

13. TV critic Tom Shales called this TV movie "beyond reprehensible as a piece
    of entertainment."[141]
    A. *You Are the Jury*
    B. *On Trial: Lee Harvey Oswald*
    C. *Oswald vs Texas*
    D. *The Trial of Lee Harvey Oswald*

14. Name the real-life Dallas Police officer who had a minor role in the CBS telemovie *Ruby and Oswald*.
    A. Jim Leavelle
    B. Luke Mooney
    C. Eugene Boone
    D. Seymour Weitzman

15. In the first season of this animated TV series, Mr. Garrison attempted to assassinate Kathie Lee Gifford from a book depository *à la* Lee Harvey Oswald.
    A. *Family Guy*
    B. *South Park*
    C. *Gravity Falls*
    D. *Bob's Burgers*

16. A former US senator from Virginia, he played the Kennedy-like president in *Winter Kills*.
    A. Paul Nitze
    B. John Warner
    C. Fred Norwich
    D. John Lehman

17. This long-running BBC program premiered the day after JFK's murder.
    A. *Dr. Who*
    B. *Monty Python*
    C. *Songs of Praise*
    D. *Above Suspicion*

18. In 1966, pop culture icon Andy Warhol directed and produced this offbeat interpretation of the Kennedy assassination.
    A. *Since*
    B. *Tiger Morse*
    C. *Lee and Jack*
    D. *Imitation of Christ*

19. During the trial sequence in *JFK*, which phrase did District Attorney Jim Garrison (Kevin Costner) repeat over and over?
    A. "You must convict."
    B. "Oswald is innocent."
    C. "Study the evidence."
    D. "Back and to the left."

20. A CBS Sports documentary, it examined the impact of JFK's death on one of college football's greatest rivalries.
    A. *JFK Memorialized: USC-Notre Dame*
    B. *The Halls of Ivy: Harvard vs. Princeton*
    C. *Titans in November: Buckeyes vs. Spartans*
    D. *Marching On: 1963 Army-Navy Remembered*

21. He starred in, codirected, and coproduced *11.22.63.*
    A. Chris Cooper
    B. James Franco
    C. Bradley Cooper
    D. James Badge Dale

22. The following actors have portrayed Jack Ruby *except* _____.
    A. Paul Carr
    B. Danny Aiello
    C. Michael Lerner
    D. Casey Siemaszko

23. In *Executive Action*, which conspirator was initially reluctant to have JFK assassinated?
    A. Robert Foster
    B. Warren Halliday
    C. Peter Huddleston
    D. Harold Ferguson

24. This 2002 cult classic featured a nursing home resident obsessed with the Kennedy murder.
    A. *Baba Looey*
    B. *Hairspray*
    C. *Bubba Ho-Tep*
    D. *The Rocky Horror Picture Show*

25. In *Winter Kills*, it was not Dealey Plaza where President Timothy Kegan was assassinated but _____.
    A. Hunt Plaza
    B. Liberty Plaza
    C. Franklin Plaza
    D. Centennial Plaza

26. Which movie's tagline was, "Her life began when her world fell apart"?[142]
    A. *Love Field*
    B. *Marina: A Life*
    C. *The Kennedys*
    D. *Jacqueline Kennedy Onassis*

27. A PBS documentary, it used state-of-the-art forensics to "solve" President Kennedy's assassination.
    A. *NCIS: Dallas*
    B. *Cold Case: JFK*
    C. *Dallas Crossfire*
    D. *Crime of the Century*

28. Best known for his starring role on *Bonanza*, he was Lee Harvey Oswald's attorney in the TV drama *The Trial of Lee Harvey Oswald*.
    A. Dan Blocker
    B. Lorne Greene
    C. Pernell Roberts
    D. Michael Landon

29. This semiregular on *Seinfeld* was also a cast member in *JFK*.
    A. Jerry Stiller
    B. Wayne Knight
    C. Norman Brenner
    D. Michael Richards

30. Name the highest grossing film at the box office.
    A. *Ruby*
    B. *Jackie*
    C. *Love Field*
    D. *Murder in Dallas*

31. In which of the following did Helena Bonham Carter star as Marina Oswald?
    A. *Final Verdict: Marina Oswald*
    B. *Presumed Guilty: Mrs. Lee Harvey Oswald*
    C. *Soviet Agent: Marina Oswald*
    D. *Fatal Deception: Mrs. Lee Harvey Oswald*

32. She portrayed country music legend Loretta Lynn in *Coal Miner's Daughter* and Mrs. Jim Garrison in *JFK*.
    A. Sally Field
    B. Jodie Foster
    C. Sissy Spacek
    D. Holly Hunter

33. Coproduced by Kate Griendling, the granddaughter of Detective Jim Leavelle, this 2013 History Channel documentary provided a fresh perspective on the arrest and capture of President Kennedy's alleged assassin.
    A. *Capturing Oswald*
    B. *Oswald: Manhunt for a Killer*
    C. *Searching for Lee Harvey Oswald*
    D. *Tracking the Man Who Murdered JFK*

34. He was the *X-Files* actor who played the part of Officer J. D. Tippit in Ruby.
    A. Mitch Pileggi
    B. Robert Patrick
    C. David Duchovny
    D. William B. Davis

35. It was the Warren Commission-like body depicted in *Winter Kills*.
    A. Church Commission
    B. Morrow Commission
    C. Pickering Commission
    D. Swanson Commission

36. Which TV sitcom featured a parody of the Magic Bullet Theory?
    A. *Friends*
    B. *Seinfeld*
    C. *Two and a Half Men*
    D. *Everybody Loves Raymond*

37. The name of JFK's assassin in *Flashpoint* was _____.
    A. Kyle W. Moffitt
    B. Michael J. Curtis
    C. Vance X. Willoughby
    D. Mitchell O. Linkletter

38. In *11.22.63*, Jake Epping is transported back to 1960 via a portal located in a _____.
    A. diner
    B. tavern
    C. hospital
    D. warehouse

39. Which *Executive Action* star succumbed to lung cancer four months before the film's theatrical release?
   A. Will Geer
   B. Robert Ryan
   C. Walter Brooke
   D. Burt Lancaster

40. As an eight-year-old boy, this future actor and narrator of the National Geographic documentary *JFK: The Final Hours*, witnessed President Kennedy's last public appearance in Fort Worth, Texas, on November 22, 1963.
   A. Bill Paxton
   B. Jeff Bridges
   C. Bill Pullman
   D. Michael Keaton

41. Who was the Emmy Award–winning actor that provided the opening narration in *JFK*?
   A. Martin Sheen
   B. William Daniels
   C. Richard Dreyfuss
   D. James Earl Jones

42. This was the tagline for the miniseries *The Kennedys*. [143]
   A. "The story behind the story"
   B. "The men. The women. Their greatness"
   C. "The triumphs and tragedies of America's greatest family"
   D. None of the above

43. In the 1951 film *The Tall Target*, a New York City detective uncovers a plot to assassinate President-elect Abraham Lincoln. What was the detective's name?
   A. Jack Ruby
   B. Lee Oswald
   C. John Kennedy
   D. Lyndon Johnson

44. Name the character in *Fatal Deception: Mrs. Lee Harvey Oswald* who said, "I can only conclude that he wanted in some way to be outstanding." [144]
    A. Ruth Paine
    B. Marina Oswald
    C. Buell Wesley Frazier
    D. Marguerite Oswald

45. This British-produced documentary purported that three French hitmen assassinated JFK.
    A. *JFK's Assassins*
    B. *Dallas Kill Zone*
    C. *Kennedy's Contract*
    D. *The Men Who Killed Kennedy*

46. In *Bubba Ho-Tep*, Jack kept a scale model of (the) _____ in his room.
    A. Love Field
    B. Dealey Plaza
    C. Texas Theater
    D. JFK's limousine

47. Who was originally cast to play the title role in *Ruby*?
    A. Joe Pesci
    B. Al Pacino
    C. Bob Hoskins
    D. Harvey Keitel

48. In this episode of *The Simpsons* there are references to the "grassy knoll" and Dallas Police Detective Jim Leavelle.
    A. "Colonel Homer"
    B. "Mayored to the Mob"
    C. "Last Exit to Springfield"
    D. "Mr. Lisa Goes to Washington"

49. The character Joe Diamond in *Winter Kills* is a fictional representation of which real-life figure?
    A. Jack Ruby
    B. David Ferrie
    C. Lyndon Johnson
    D. Lee Harvey Oswald

50. Based on the 1976 book by Robert Groden and F. Peter Model, this documentary examined the photographic evidence surrounding JFK's death.
    A. *Dark Day in Dallas*
    B. *Murder on Elm Street*
    C. *Rendezvous with Oswald*
    D. *JFK: The Case for Conspiracy*

51. "When you fight the past, the past fights back" was the tagline for the miniseries _____.[145]
    A. *11.22.63*
    B. *Time Traveler*
    C. *Back to the Future*
    D. *Remembering Dallas*

52. In this short film by Irish director Paul Duane, a group of friends recreated the JFK assassination at a dinner party.
    A. *Separate Tables*
    B. *My Dinner with Andre*
    C. *Supper with Jack Ruby*
    D. *My Dinner with Oswald*

53. Best known for his performances in *Cinderella Man* and *John Adams*, he portrayed Abraham Zapruder in *Parkland*.
    A. David Morse
    B. Paul Giamatti
    C. Russell Crowe
    D. Tom Wilkinson

54. Which make and model car did Jake Epping drive in *11.22.63*?
    A. Buick Riviera
    B. Ford Fairlane
    C. Chevy Impala
    D. Oldsmobile Cutlass

55. Name the *Saturday Night Live* alumnus who took the role of Jack Ruby in *JFK*.
    A. John Candy
    B. Chevy Chase
    C. Dan Ackroyd
    D. Brian Doyle-Murray

56. He starred as Lee Harvey Oswald in both the motion picture *Ruby* and the TV series *Quantum Leap*.
    A. Kevin Turner
    B. Bruce Wright
    C. Stephen Lane
    D. Willie Garson

57. "One conspiracy leads to another" was the tagline for _____.[146]
    A. *Killing Kennedy*
    B. *Ruby and Oswald*
    C. *Conspiracy Games*
    D. *Assassination Tango*

58. Which actor from *In the Line of Fire* said, "I see you standing over the grave of another dead president"?[147]
    A. Rene Russo
    B. Clint Eastwood
    C. John Malkovich
    D. Dylan McDermott

59. Released in 1969, this "Spaghetti Western" depicted the death of President James Garfield with references to the Kennedy assassination.

A. *Vengeance Is Mine*

B. *The Price of Power*

C. *Dead Men Don't Count*

D. *For a Few Dollars More*

60. An Oscar-winning actor and producer, he provided the narration for the documentary *JFK: One P.M. Central Standard Time*.

A. Tom Hanks

B. Jeff Bridges

C. Ben Kingsley

D. George Clooney

61. Directed by Henri Verneuil, this French film explored the conspiracy theories surrounding the assassination of President Kennedy.

A. *I...For Icarus*

B. *Outside the Law*

C. *Section Speciale*

D. *The Day of the Jackal*

62. "The story that won't go away" was the tagline for the film _____.[148]

A. *JFK*

B. *Dateline Dallas*

C. *Ruby and Oswald*

D. *Contract Assassins*

63. In *Killing Kennedy*, who was the character that said, "Anybody who bumps that bastard off would be doing the world a favor."[149]

A. J. Edgar Hoover

B. Robert Kennedy

C. Lee Harvey Oswald

D. George de Mohrenschildt

64. Which two assassination-based films took place in the "City of Brotherly Love"?
   A. *Blowout* and *Winter Kills*
   B. *The Parallax View* and *Blonde*
   C. *The Butler* and *The Parallax View*
   D. *Winter Kills* and *Assassination Tango*

65. In the second season of this sci-fi drama, time travellers attempted to prevent the death of JFK only to learn that he had been assassinated in Austin, Texas, in 1961.
   A. *Timeless*
   B. *Lost in Space*
   C. *Time Traveler*
   D. *Ghost Hunters*

66. Best known for his starring role on ABC's *Voyage to the Bottom of the Sea*, he narrated the 1964 Oscar-nominated documentary *Four Days in November*.
   A. Walter Pigeon
   B. David Hedison
   C. William Shatner
   D. Richard Basehart

67. The Kennedy assassination was referenced in two Nicholas Cage films. What were they?
   A. *Con Air* and *Face-Off*
   B. *Deadfall* and *The Boy in Blue*
   C. *The Rock* and *National Treasure*
   D. *Ghost Rider* and *World Trade Center*

68. On which popular 90s TV show would you find conspiracy geeks known as the "Lone Gunmen"?
   A. *The X-Files*
   B. *Marvel's Avengers*
   C. *The Big Bang Theory*
   D. *3rd Rock from the Sun*

69. "CIA, Mafia, conspiracy, Jack Ruby" was the tagline for _____.[150]
    A. *Ruby*
    B. *Mafia Gunman*
    C. *Jack Ruby: Assassin*
    D. *Ruby and Oswald*

70. Who was the Academy Award–winning actor that portrayed Lee Harvey
    Oswald in *JFK*?
    A. Colin Firth
    B. Sean Penn
    C. Gary Oldman
    D. Kevin Spacey

71. Place these films in chronological order.
    1. *JFK*
    2. *Love Field*
    3. *Executive Action*
    4. *Interview with the Assassin*
    A. 2., 4., 1., 3.
    B. 1., 3., 4., 2.
    C. 3., 1., 2., 4.
    D. 4., 2., 1., 3.

72. Name the 2008 PBS documentary based on the book of the same name by
    Pulitzer Prize–winning author Norman Mailer.
    A. *Oswald's Ghost*
    B. *Oswald's Fiasco*
    C. *Oswald's Specter*
    D. *Oswald's Dilemma*

73. *On the Trail of the Assassin* and *Crossfire: The Plot That Killed Kennedy* were the basis for which film?
    A. *JFK*
    B. *Murder Inc.*
    C. *Eye of the Assassin*
    D. *An American Crime*

74. What did Jake Epping do for a living in *11.22.63*?
    A. Used car salesman
    B. Grocery store clerk
    C. State police officer
    D. High school teacher

75. In this two-part episode of *Quantum Leap*, Dr. Sam Beckett entered the body of Lee Harvey Oswald.
    A. "Camelot"
    B. "Kill Zone"
    C. "Day of Days"
    D. "Lee Harvey Oswald"

76. All of these films were Oscar-nominated *except* _____.
    A. *JFK*
    B. *Ruby*
    C. *Jackie*
    D. *Love Field*

77. Veteran actor Ben Gazzara played the prosecutor in the TV docudrama
    _____.
    A. *Oswald: Assassin or Fall Guy*
    B. *The Trial of Lee Harvey Oswald*
    C. *Lee Harvey Oswald: Presumed Guilty*
    D. *Guilt by Association: Lee Harvey Oswald*

78. This was the tagline for *Interview with the Assassin*.[151]
    A. "This man killed JFK"
    B. "One man did not act alone"
    C. "Dallas, 1963: The second shooter"
    D. "Could he really be the other gunman?"

79. Which German-produced documentary concluded that elements of the Cuban government planned the assassination of President Kennedy?
    A. *Murder for Hire*
    B. *Assassination Tango*
    C. *Rendezvous with Death*
    D. *Who Killed the President?*

80. A future US senator, he played presidential chief of staff Harry Sargent in *In the Line of Fire*.
    A. Fred Grandy
    B. Ralph Waite
    C. Fred Thompson
    D. Noble Willingham

81. Name the Austrian-born actor who narrated the German-language version of *John F. Kennedy: Years of Lightning, Day of Drums*.
    A. Curt Jurgens
    B. Max von Sydow
    C. Jan Josef Liefers
    D. Maximillian Schell

82. "James Farrington, heart attack, Parkland Hospital" was the final line from which movie?[152]
    A. *Parallax View*
    B. *Executive Action*
    C. *The Quiller Memorandum*
    D. *Interview with the Assassin*

83. "The Assassination of President Kennedy" was an episode of this CNN series.
    A. *The Sixties*
    B. *American Assassins*
    C. *The Turbulent Decade*
    D. *Historical Turning Points*

84. Who was the voice of Lee Harvey Oswald in the PBS documentary *Frontline: Who Was Lee Harvey Oswald?*
    A. Willie Garson
    B. Gary Oldman
    C. John Pleshette
    D. Robert Downey Jr.

85. Before appearing in *JFK*, this acting duo starred in *The Fortune Cookie* and *The Odd Couple*.
    A. Gene Hackman and Roy Scheider
    B. Paul Newman and Robert Redford
    C. Walter Matthau and Jack Lemmon
    D. Elliot Gould and Donald Sutherland

86. In which 2016 episode of *Hawaii Five-O* did an assassination researcher uncover evidence that JFK's cabinet arranged his murder?
    A. "Pono Kaulike" ("Justice for All")
    B. "E ʻImi pono" ("Searching for the Truth")
    C. "Hauʻoli La HoʻomaikaʻI" ("Happy Thanksgiving")
    D. "Elua la ma Nowemapa" ("Two Days in November")

87. Actor and writer Gary Grubbs appeared in two JFK assassination films. Name them.
    A. *JFK* and *Parkland*
    B. *Flashpoint* and *Ruby*
    C. *Executive Action* and *JFK*
    D. *Parkland* and *Love Field*

88. In *X-Men: Days of Future Past*, it was revealed that _____ had been imprisoned for his alleged role in the Kennedy assassination.
    A. Magneto
    B. Deadpool
    C. Wolverine
    D. Professor X

89. This *West Wing* actor played JFK on the TV miniseries *Kennedy*.
    A. Martin Sheen
    B. Tim Matheson
    C. Timothy Busfield
    D. Bradley Whitford

90. "On November 22, 1963, President John F. Kennedy was assassinated. This is the story of what happened next" was the tagline for _____.[153]
    A. *LBJ*
    B. *RFK*
    C. *Ruby*
    D. *Parkland*

91. A two-time Oscar winner, he narrated the 2013 documentary *The Day Kennedy Died*.
    A. Kevin Spacey
    B. Robert De Niro
    C. Dustin Hoffman
    D. Michael Douglas

92. This film was adapted from the best-selling book by attorney and Warren Commission critic Mark Lane.
    A. *Eternal Vigilance*
    B. *A Citizen's Dissent*
    C. *Murder Most Foul*
    D. *Rush to Judgement*

93. For which movie did Tommy Lee Jones receive his first Academy Award nomination?
    A. *JFK*
    B. *Ruby*
    C. *Winter Kills*
    D. *Deadline Dallas*

94. Featured in the World War l film *1917*, he played Bill Turcotte in *11.22.63*.
    A. Michael Strong
    B. George MacKay
    C. Benedict Cumberbatch
    D. Dean-Charles Chapman

95. In this *X-Files* episode, we learned who killed JFK.
    A. "The Field Where I Died"
    B. "Nightmare on Elm Street"
    C. "The Single Bullet Theory"
    D. "Musings of a Cigarette Man"

96. All of the following have portrayed Lee Harvey Oswald *except* _____.
    A. Will Rothhaar
    B. Trevor Burton
    C. Jeremy Strong
    D. Frederic Forrest

97. His screenplay was the basis for *Interview with the Assassin*.
    A. Neil Burger
    B. Stephen Brewer
    C. Richard Sizemore
    D. Mitchell Washington

98. Who was the Academy Award–winning actor that narrated the English-language version of *John F. Kennedy: Years of Lightning, Day of Drums*?
    A. Peter Finch
    B. Gregory Peck
    C. Ernest Borgnine
    D. Charlton Heston

99. The son of a Hollywood legend, he played Dr. Malcolm Perry in *Parkland*.
    A. Colin Hanks
    B. Ray Nicholson
    C. Scott Eastwood
    D. Kiefer Sutherland

100. On the Netflix series *The Umbrella Academy*, which member of the Hargreaves family became obsessed with preventing the Kennedy assassination?
    A. Diego
    B. Vanya
    C. Luther
    D. Allison

CHAPTER NINE ANSWERS

1.   A. Dalton Trumbo
2.   B. Jim Garrison and Robert Groden
3.   D. *The JFK Assassination: The Jim Garrison Tapes*
4.   B. Greg Kinnear
5.   A. *Psycho*
6.   D. Kris Kristofferson
7.   C. *Interview with the Assassin*
8.   D. Frank Whaley
9.   C. Henry Gibson
10.   D. "If they can knock off a president, they can knock off the president of a union."
11.   B. Rachel Weisz
12.   B. Mel Gibson and Harrison Ford
13.   D. *The Trial of Lee Harvey Oswald*
14.   A. Jim Leavelle
15.   B. *South Park*
16.   B. John Warner
17.   A. *Dr. Who*
18.   A. *Since*
19.   D. "Back and to the left."
20.   D. *Marching On: 1963 Army-Navy Remembered*
21.   B. James Franco
22.   A. Paul Carr
23.   D. Harold Ferguson
24.   C. *Bubba Ho-Tep*
25.   A. Hunt Plaza
26.   A. *Love Field*
27.   B. *Cold Case: JFK*
28.   B. Lorne Greene
29.   B. Wayne Knight
30.   B. *Jackie*
31.   D. *Fatal Deception: Mrs. Lee Harvey Oswald*

32. C. Sissy Spacek
33. A. *Capturing Oswald*
34. C. David Duchovny
35. C. Pickering Commission
36. B. *Seinfeld*
37. B. Michael J. Curtis
38. A. diner
39. B. Robert Ryan
40. A. Bill Paxton
41. A. Martin Sheen
42. C. "The triumphs and tragedies of America's greatest family"
43. C. John Kennedy
44. D. Marguerite Oswald
45. D. *The Men Who Killed Kennedy*
46. B. Dealey Plaza
47. C. Bob Hoskins
48. B. "Mayored to the Mob"
49. A. Jack Ruby
50. D. *JFK: The Case for Conspiracy*
51. A. *11/22/63*
52. D. *My Dinner with Oswald*
53. B. Paul Giamatti
54. B. Ford Fairlane
55. D. Brian Doyle-Murray
56. D. Willie Garson
57. B. *Ruby and Oswald*
58. C. John Malkovich
59. B. *The Price of Power*
60. D. George Clooney
61. A. *I...For Icarus*
62. A. *JFK*
63. D. George de Mohrenschildt
64. A. *Blowout and Winter Kills*
65. A. *Timeless*
66. D. Richard Basehart

67. C. *The Rock* and *National Treasure*
68. A. *The X-Files*
69. A. *Ruby*
70. C. Gary Oldman
71. C. 3., 1., 2., 4.
72. A. *Oswald's Ghost*
73. A. *JFK*
74. D. High school teacher
75. D. "Lee Harvey Oswald"
76. B. *Ruby*
77. B. *The Trial of Lee Harvey Oswald*
78. C. "Dallas, 1963: The second shooter"
79. C. *Rendezvous with Death*
80. C. Fred Thompson
81. D. Maximillian Schell
82. B. *Executive Action*
83. A. *The Sixties*
84. B. Gary Oldman
85. C. Walter Matthau and Jack Lemmon
86. D. "Elua la ma Nowemapa" ("Two Days in November")
87. A. *JFK* and *Parkland*
88. A. Magneto
89. A. Martin Sheen
90. D. *Parkland*
91. A. Kevin Spacey
92. D. *Rush to Judgement*
93. A. *JFK*
94. B. George McKay
95. D. "Musings of a Cigarette Man"
96. B. Trevor Burton
97. C. Richard Sizemore
98. B. Gregory Peck
99. A. Colin Hanks
100. A. Diego

CHAPTER TEN

1963: THE YEAR IN REVIEW

1. Which of these astronauts piloted *Faith 7*, the final mission of Project Mercury?
   A. John Glenn
   B. Gordon Cooper
   C. Donald Slayton
   D. Scott Carpenter

2. Nicknamed "The Golden Bear," he defeated a legendary field of golfers to win the twenty-seventh Masters Tournament.
   A. Sam Snead
   B. Gene Sarazen
   C. Jack Nicklaus
   D. Arnold Palmer

3. At his gubernatorial inauguration he declared, "Segregation now, segregation tomorrow, segregation forever!"[154]
   A. Fritz Hollings
   B. Orval Faubus
   C. Lester Maddox
   D. George Wallace

4. The price of a US postage stamp was increased to _____.
   A. two cents
   B. five cents
   C. eight cents
   D. twelve cents

5. Who was the Soviet cosmonaut that became the first woman in space?
    A. Yelena Serova
    B. Marina Kondakova
    C. Svetlana Savitskaya
    D. Valentina Tereshkova

6. Featuring an ensemble cast, this film was awarded the Golden Globe for Best Motion Picture by the Hollywood Foreign Press Association.
    A. *The Longest Day*
    B. *Lawrence of Arabia*
    C. *The Chapman Report*
    D. *Mutiny on the Bounty*

7. Dr. Martin Luther King Jr. delivered his "I Have a Dream" speech in which of the following cities?
    A. Washington, DC
    B. Richmond, Virginia
    C. Memphis, Tennessee
    D. Birmingham, Alabama

8. Legendary vocalist Tony Bennett's signature song, it won the Grammy Award for Best Record of the Year.
    A. "Rags to Riches"
    B. "Because of You"
    C. "Put On a Happy Face"
    D. "I Left My Heart in San Francisco"

9. Cardinal Giovanni Montini (Paul VI) was elected to the papacy following the death of _____.
    A. Leo VX
    B. Pius XII
    C. John XXIII
    D. Constantine II

10. Unquestionably the greatest St. Louis Cardinal of all time and baseball's definition of consistency, he retired with 3,630 career hits, 475 home runs, 1,951 RBIs, and a lifetime batting average of .331.
A. Ken Boyer
B. Curt Flood
C. Stan Musial
D. Rogers Hornsby

11. The estimated population of the US was _____.
A. 157,000,000
B. 162,000,000
C. 175,000,000
D. 189,000,000

12. American novelist and civil rights activist James Baldwin published this best-selling book about racial injustice in America.
A. *Giovanni's Room*
B. *The Fire Next Time*
C. *Nobody Knows My Name*
D. *Go Tell It on the Mountain*

13. In which US museum was Leonardo da Vinci's painting of the Mona Lisa exhibited for the first time?
A. Guggenheim Museum
B. National Gallery of Art
C. Rosencrans Art Institute
D. Metropolitan Museum of Art

14. All of the following vehicles debuted *except* _____.
A. Porsche 911
B. Jeep Wagoneer
C. Plymouth Duster
D. Corvette Sting Ray

15. ZIP codes were introduced by the US Postal Service. ZIP is an acronym for
    _____.
    A. Zero Issue Program
    B. Zone Improvement Plan
    C. Zero Issuance Procedure
    D. Zone Institution Plan

16. "Please Please Me" was the first single released in the US by this British
    group.
    A. The Beatles
    B. The Animals
    C. The Zombies
    D. The Quarrymen

17. A Soviet military officer, he was convicted and executed for passing over
    five thousand classified documents to American and British intelligence.
    A. Dmitri Polyakov
    B. Ivan Susloparov
    C. Oleg Penkovsky
    D. Gregor Tupolov

18. Her portrayal of Helen Keller in the motion picture *The Miracle Worker*
    earned _____ the Oscar for Best Supporting Actress.
    A. Patty Duke
    B. Jane Fonda
    C. Natalie Wood
    D. Anne Bancroft

19. This Category Four hurricane ravaged the Caribbean, inflicting nearly
    7,200 deaths.
    A. Kay
    B. Luke
    C. Flora
    D. Steve

20. Which future US president played the piano on *The Jack Paar Program?*
   A. Jimmy Carter
   B. Richard Nixon
   C. Barack Obama
   D. Ronald Reagan

21. In what became known as the Profumo Affair, British Secretary of State for War John Profumo was forced to resign after he engaged in a sexual liaison with a nineteen-year-old model. Who was she?
   A. Christine Keeler
   B. Margaret Porter
   C. Bonnie Duckworth
   D. Constance Middleton

22. This motorcycle manufacturer said in their ad "Just add a gallon of gas and you're ready to go 225 miles."
   A. Honda
   B. Suzuki
   C. Yamaha
   D. Triumph

23. A renowned research scientist, he performed the first liver transplant at the University of Colorado.
   A. Victor Chang
   B. Jules Bernard
   C. Thomas Starzl
   D. Magnus Olsen

24. Which American Football League franchise relocated to the Midwest and became the Kansas City Chiefs?
   A. Dallas Texans
   B. Houston Oilers
   C. Boston Patriots
   D. New York Titans

25. JFK increased the number of US troops in Vietnam from 11,000 to _____.
    A. 12,500
    B. 13,000
    C. 14,500
    D. 16,000

26. Sung by Kyu Sakamoto, it was the first and last Japanese song to top the
    Billboard Hot 100.
    A. "Ichizu"
    B. "Sukiyaki"
    C. "Homura"
    D. "Torisetsu"

27. The US Supreme Court ruled in _____ that every person is entitled to
    legal representation regardless of their circumstances.
    A. *Fay v. Noia*
    B. *Wright v. Georgia*
    C. *Jones v. Cunningham*
    D. *Gideon v. Wainwright*

28. Known as "The Greatest Spectacle in Racing," the forty-seventh
    Indianapolis 500 was won by _____.
    A. Eddie Sachs
    B. Dan Gurney
    C. Rodger Ward
    D. Parnelli Jones

29. A devastating earthquake destroyed the city of Skopje in this European
    country.
    A. Greece
    B. Romania
    C. Yugoslavia
    D. Czechoslovakia

30. For his performance in *Lilies of the Field*, he became the first African American to win an Academy Award for Best Actor.
    A. Brock Peters
    B. Sidney Poitier
    C. Harry Belafonte
    D. James Earl Jones

31. The Viet Cong secured their first major victory of the Vietnam War at the _____.
    A. Battle of Hue
    B. Battle of Ap Bac
    C. Battle of Binh Gia
    D. Battle of Khe Sanh

32. Which automobile advertisement claimed that their vehicle delivered more power?
    A. Mercury Monterey
    B. Lincoln Continental
    C. Plymouth Belvedere
    D. Chrysler New Yorker

33. President Sylvanus Olympio was assassinated during a political coup in the West African country of _____.
    A. Togo
    B. Liberia
    C. Guinea
    D. Sierra Leone

34. The price of a movie ticket at your neighborhood theater was _____.
    A. ten cents
    B. fifteen cents
    C. sixty-two cents
    D. eighty-five cents

35. Commissioned in 1961, this US nuclear-powered attack submarine sank during diving tests some two hundred miles east of Cape Cod, Massachusetts.
    A. U.S.S. *Nautilus*
    B. U.S.S. *Thresher*
    C. U.S.S. *Neptune*
    D. U.S.S. *Los Angeles*

36. A tube of Crest toothpaste was _____.
    A. fifty cents
    B. sixty cents
    C. eighty cents
    D. ninety cents

37. Colloquially referred to as the "hotline," the _____ established a communication link between Washington and Moscow.
    A. Mutual Defense Communications Pact
    B. International Communication and Control Treaty
    C. East-West Bilateral Strategic Arms Limitation Pact
    D. Washington-Moscow Direct Communications Link

38. The following celebrities were born *except* _____.
    A. Brad Pitt
    B. Lisa Kudrow
    C. Vanessa Williams
    D. Robert Downey Jr.

39. Authorized by the US Congress, this coin honored slain President John F. Kennedy.
    A. Penny
    B. Nickle
    C. Quarter
    D. Half dollar

40. Which team defeated the Detroit Red Wings to capture the Stanley Cup?

    A. Boston Bruins

    B. Montreal Canadians

    C. Toronto Maple Leafs

    D. Chicago Black Hawks

41. The Catholic Church allowed this practice to take place.

    A. Baptism

    B. Cremation

    C. Reconciliation

    D. Anointing of the sick

42. Name the legendary British TV series that aired for the first time.

    A. *Brideshead Revisited*

    B. *Monty Python's Flying Circus*

    C. *That Was the Week That Was*

    D. None of the above

43. JFK delivered his "Ich bin ein Berliner" speech at this symbol of Soviet oppression.

    A. Berlin Wall

    B. Reichstag Building

    C. Brandenburg Gate

    D. Neuschwanstein Castle

44. A Frigidaire portable air conditioner cost _____.

    A. $104

    B. $115

    C. $149

    D. $170

45. In London, seventy thousand people demonstrated against _____.
    A. racism
    B. hunger
    C. genocide
    D. nuclear weapons

46. He became the second-oldest golfer to win the US Open.
    A. Art Wall
    B. Dick Mayer
    C. Julius Boros
    D. Bobby Locke

47. An influential force in country music, she died in a Tennessee plane crash.
    A. Patsy Cline
    B. Kittie Wells
    C. Jean Shepard
    D. Cindy Walker

48. Three of Albert DeSalvo's thirteen female victims were murdered in 1963. Better-known as the "Boston Strangler," he was originally dubbed the _____.
    A. "Phantom Fiend"
    B. "Maniacal Menace"
    C. "Charlestown Cuckoo"
    D. "Scourge of Dorchester"

49. Known as "The Most Famous Train in the World," it was finally retired after thirty-five years of service.
    A. *Guardsman*
    B. *Royal Majestic*
    C. *London Express*
    D. *Flying Scotsman*

50. According to Nielsen Media Research, the year's top-rated TV show was
_____.
A. *The Ed Sullivan Show*
B. *The Beverly Hillbillies*
C. *The Dick Van Dyke Show*
D. *The Adventures of Ozzie and Harriet*

51. Which Southeast Asian leader was assassinated during a military coup
d'état some three weeks before the death of President Kennedy?
A. Bao Dai
B. Ngo Dinh Diem
C. Duong Van Minh
D. Tran Thien Khiem

52. A gallon of gasoline cost _____.
A. fifteen cents
B. eighteen cents
C. twenty-two cents
D. twenty-nine cents

53. This civil rights icon became the first African American to graduate from
the University of Mississippi.
A. Jesse Jackson
B. Ralph Bunche
C. James Meredith
D. Cleve McDowell

54. A cinematic epic, it was the highest grossing film of the year.
A. *The Birds*
B. *Cleopatra*
C. *The Great Escape*
D. *How the West Was Won*

55. Civil rights protestors were attacked with water cannons and police dogs in the city of _____.
   A. Savannah, Georgia
   B. Nashville, Tennessee
   C. Birmingham, Alabama
   D. Raleigh, North Carolina

56. This French cyclist won the Tour de France for the third consecutive year.
   A. Laurent Fignon
   B. Pierre Barbotin
   C. Jacques Anquetil
   D. Thomas Voeckler

57. NASA test pilot Joseph Walker established the world altitude record in the _____.
   A. X-10
   B. X-15
   C. X-19
   D. X-22

58. Which company introduced the first push-button telephone?
   A. Bell Telephone
   B. Deutsche Telekom
   C. Edison Field Communications
   D. New York Telephone and Telegraph

59. The US prohibited all monetary transactions with this country.
   A. Cuba
   B. Portugal
   C. Argentina
   D. Soviet Union

60. Released in movie theaters five months before the assassination, *PT-109* starred _____ as the future thirty-fifth president.
    A. Ty Hardin
    B. Robert Culp
    C. Warren Beatty
    D. Cliff Robertson

61. This famed rock band made its British TV debut on *Thank Your Lucky Stars.*
    A. Queen
    B. Pink Floyd
    C. Black Sabbath
    D. None of the above

62. A Hershey's chocolate bar cost _____.
    A. five cents
    B. eleven cents
    C. fifteen cents
    D. twenty-five cents

63. It was the first organization to speak out against the dangers of smoking.
    A. World Health Board
    B. American Red Cross
    C. International Health Agency
    D. American Heart Association

64. Known as "The Most Exciting Two Minutes in Sports," the eighty-ninth Kentucky Derby was won by _____.
    A. Never Bend
    B. Chateaugay
    C. War Admiral
    D. On My Honor

65. A protectorate of Great Britain, it gained its independence and later became a member of the East African Community.
    A. Kenya
    B. Somalia
    C. Ethiopia
    D. Botswana

66. They were the first networks to move to a thirty-minute evening news format.
    A. ABC and CBS
    B. CBS and NBC
    C. ABC and CNN
    D. NBC and PBS

67. JFK called it morally wrong and said that "the time to act" is now.
    A. Poverty
    B. Illiteracy
    C. Segregation
    D. Communism

68. This influential musician scored a *Billboard* hit with the novelty instrumental "Yakety Sax."
    A. Buck Owens
    B. Pete Fountain
    C. Boots Randolph
    D. Cannonball Adderley

69. It was the first state in the Union to establish a lottery.
    A. California
    B. Mississippi
    C. South Carolina
    D. New Hampshire

70. The political thriller *Seven Days in May* was published by Harper & Row. Who was the author?

A. Tom Clancy

B. Fletcher Knebel

C. Richard Condon

D. Frederick Forsyth

71. A sixty-six-year-old Vietnamese monk, Thich Quang Duc, committed self-immolation to protest government policies against Buddhists. In which city did the incident occur?

A. Hanoi

B. Pleiku

C. Saigon

D. Haiphong

72. One of JFK's all-time favorite books, it was adapted for the screen and the last film he watched before his trip to Texas.

A. *Pilgrim's Way*

B. *The Price of Union*

C. *From Russia with Love*

D. *The Man Who Never Was*

73. This infamous federal penitentiary in San Francisco, California, was permanently closed.

A. Folsom

B. Alcatraz

C. Sing Sing

D. Rikers Island

74. All of the following toys were manufactured by Mattel *except* _____.

A. G.I. Joe

B. Chatty Cathy

C. Easy-Bake Oven

D. Cecil the Seasick Serpent

75. He stepped down as prime minister of Israel.
    A. Levi Eshkol
    B. Ariel Sharon
    C. David Ben-Gurion
    D. Menachem Begin

76. The quarterback for the US Naval Academy, he was only the second midshipman to win the prestigious Heisman Trophy.
    A. Bob Griese
    B. Ken Stabler
    C. Terry Bradshaw
    D. Roger Staubach

77. Alec Douglas-Home became British prime minister following the resignation of _____.
    A. Edward Heath
    B. Harold Wilson
    C. Winston Churchill
    D. Harold Macmillan

78. The following celebrities died *except* _____.
    A. Walt Disney
    B. Robert Frost
    C. Aldous Huxley
    D. W. E. B. Du Bois

79. In this landmark case, the US Supreme Court ruled that prayer in schools was unconstitutional.
    A. *Oklahoma v. Smith*
    B. *Washington v. Twitchell High School*
    C. *Abington School District v. Schempp*
    D. *Miller v. Bucks County Board of Education*

80. The New York Giants defeated the _____ 14–10 to capture the thirty-first NFL championship.
    A. Chicago Bears
    B. Minnesota Vikings
    C. Green Bay Packers
    D. Philadelphia Eagles

81. A member of British intelligence, he defected to the Soviet Union.
    A. Kim Philby
    B. Trevor Martin
    C. Roger Evanston
    D. Mitchell Willoughby

82. "We Try Harder" was the advertising slogan for which airline?
    A. TWA
    B. United
    C. Eastern
    D. None of the above

83. Jacqueline Kennedy became the first first lady to give birth while serving in the White House since _____.
    A. Lou Hoover
    B. Edith Wilson
    C. Grace Coolidge
    D. Frances Cleveland

84. The average price of a new home was _____.
    A. $16,500
    B. $19,000
    C. $20,500
    D. $21,000

85. Zanzibar gained independence from which former colonial power?
    A. Italy
    B. Spain
    C. France
    D. Great Britain

86. Led by Bob Cousy and Bill Russell, the Boston Celtics won their fourth straight NBA championship by defeating the _____.
    A. Detroit Pistons
    B. St. Louis Hawks
    C. Los Angeles Lakers
    D. San Francisco Warriors

87. According to the National Weather Bureau, this city experienced the seventh largest snowfall in history.
    A. Cleveland, Ohio
    B. Detroit, Michigan
    C. New York, New York
    D. Green Bay, Wisconsin

88. Hosted by Monty Hall, this perennial game show premiered on NBC.
    A. *Jeopardy*
    B. *You Don't Say*
    C. *Wheel of Fortune*
    D. *Let's Make a Deal*

89. An antiapartheid leader and future president of South Africa, he was tried and convicted of crimes against the government.
    A. Jacob Zuma
    B. Thabo Mbeki
    C. Oliver Tambo
    D. Nelson Mandela

90. This long-running soap opera debuted on ABC featuring the characters Dr. Steve Hardy and Nurse Jessie Brewer.
    A. *One Life to Live*
    B. *General Hospital*
    C. *Days of Our Lives*
    D. *The Edge of Night*

91. Which Boeing airliner made its maiden flight?
    A. 707
    B. 727
    C. 747
    D. 767

92. The average cost of a new car was _____.
    A. $3,200
    B. $3,650
    C. $3,800
    D. $3,950

93. Kusno Sosrodihardjo (Sukarno) was appointed this country's president for life.
    A. Thailand
    B. Malaysia
    C. Indonesia
    D. Timor-Leste

94. All of the following were dance crazes *except* _____.
    A. "Monkey"
    B. "Hitch Hike"
    C. "Time Warp"
    D. "Chicken Dance"

95. Frank Sinatra Jr. was abducted and ransomed by kidnappers for _____.
   A. $185,000
   B. $240,000
   C. $325,000
   D. $500,000

96. Name the ABC series that featured a doctor on the run and a one-armed killer.
   A. *Ben Casey*
   B. *The Fugitive*
   C. *Johnny Midnight*
   D. *Run for Your Life*

97. The Elysée Treaty was signed between these two European countries.
   A. Belgium and Poland
   B. Holland and Denmark
   C. France and West Germany
   D. East Germany and Sweden

98. Which of the following credit cards debuted in Great Britain?
   A. Visa
   B. Mastercard
   C. Diner's Club
   D. American Express

99. This future Dallas Cowboy wide receiver set a world record for the hundred yard dash at the AAU track and field competition.
   A. Bob Hayes
   B. Tony Dorsett
   C. Drew Pearson
   D. Lance Rentzel

100. A French military officer, Jean Bastien-Thiry, was executed for attempting to assassinate _____.
     A. Charles de Gaulle
     B. Amintore Fanfani
     C. Georges Pompidou
     D. Valery Giscard d'Estaing

Chapter Ten Answers

1. B. Gordon Cooper
2. C. Jack Nicklaus
3. D. George Wallace
4. B. five cents
5. C. Svetlana Savitskaya
6. D. *Lawrence of Arabia*
7. A. Washington, DC
8. D. "I Left My Heart in San Francisco"
9. C. John XXIII
10. C. Stan Musial
11. D. 189,000,000
12. B. *The Fire Next Time*
13. B. National Gallery of Art
14. C. Plymouth Duster
15. B. Zone Improvement Plan
16. A. The Beatles
17. C. Oleg Penkovsky
18. A. Patty Duke
19. C. Flora
20. B. Richard Nixon
21. A. Christine Keeler
22. A. Honda
23. C. Thomas Starzl
24. A. Dallas Texans
25. D. 16,000
26. B. "Sukiyaki"
27. D. *Gideon v. Wainwright*
28. D. Parnelli Jones
29. C. Yugoslavia
30. B. Sidney Poitier
31. B. Battle of Ap Bac
32. B. Lincoln Continental

33. A. Togo
34. D. eighty-five cents
35. B. U.S.S. *Thresher*
36. A. fifty cents
37. D. Washington-Moscow Direct Communications Link
38. D. Robert Downey Jr.
39. D. Half dollar
40. C. Toronto Maple Leafs
41. B. Cremation
42. D. None of the above
43. A. Berlin Wall
44. C. $149
45. D. nuclear weapons
46. C. Julius Boros
47. A. Patsy Cline
48. A. "Phantom Fiend"
49. D. *Flying Scotsman*
50. B. The Beverly Hillbillies
51. B. Ngo Dinh Diem
52. D. twenty-nine cents
53. C. James Meredith
54. B. *Cleopatra*
55. C. Birmingham, Alabama
56. C. Jacques Anquetil
57. B. X-15
58. A. Bell Telephone
59. A. Cuba
60. D. Cliff Robertson
61. D. None of the above
62. A. five cents
63. D. American Heart Association
64. B. Chateaugay
65. A. Kenya
66. B. CBS and NBC
67. C. Segregation

68. C. Boots Randolph
69. D. New Hampshire
70. B. Fletcher Knebel
71. C. Saigon
72. C. *From Russia with Love*
73. B. Alcatraz
74. A. G.I. Joe
75. C. David Ben Gurion
76. D. Roger Staubach
77. D. Harold Macmillan
78. A. Walt Disney
79. C. *Abington School District v. Schempp*
80. A. Chicago Bears
81. A. Kim Philby
82. D. None of the above
83. D. Frances Cleveland
84. B. $19,000
85. D. Great Britain
86. C. Los Angeles Lakers
87. C. New York, New York
88. D. *Let's Make a Deal*
89. D. Nelson Mandela
90. B. General Hospital
91. B. 727
92. A. $3,200
93. C. Indonesia
94. C. "Time Warp"
95. B. $240,000
96. B. *The Fugitive*
97. C. France and West Germany
98. D. American Express
99. A. Bob Hayes
100. A. Charles de Gaulle

ORDER OF PRIMARY VEHICLES IN THE DALLAS MOTORCADE*

Advance Car
Captain Perdue Lawrence

Pilot Car
Deputy Chief George Lumpkin
Detective Faye Turner
Detective William Senkle
Lieutenant Colonel George Whitmeyer
Jacob Puterbaugh

DPD Advance Motorcycles
Sergeant S. Q. Bellah
Glen C. McBride
J. B. Garrick

---

* The motorcade also included two White House press buses, a local press pool car, a Western Union car, a White House Signal Corps car, a White House staff bus, and a DPD cruiser.

DPD Lead Motorcycles
Leon Gray
E. D. Brewer
J. B. Garrick
Stavis Ellis
W. C. Lumpkin

Lead Car
Chief Jesse Curry
SA Winston Lawson
Sheriff Bill Decker
SA Forrest Sorrels

Presidential Limousine
SA William Greer
ASAIC Roy Kellerman
Mrs. Nellie Connally
Governor John Connally
Mrs. Jacqueline Kennedy
President John F. Kennedy

DPD Motorcycles
Billy Joe Martin
James Chaney
Bobby Hargis
D.L. Jackson

US Secret Service Follow-up Car
SA Sam Kinney
ASAIC Emory Roberts
SA Clint Hill
SA John Ready
Ken O'Donnell

Dave Powers
SA George Hickey
SA Paul Landis
SA George Hickey
SA Glen Bennett

Vice Presidential Car
Hurchel Jacks, TSHP
ASAIC Rufus Youngblood
Senator Ralph Yarborough
Lady Bird Johnson
Vice President Lyndon Johnson

Vice Presidential Secret Service Follow-up Car
Joe Rich, TSHP
Cliff Carter
SA Jerry Kivell
SA Warren Taylor
SA Lem Johns

Mayor's Car
Milton Wright, TSHP
Mayor Earle Cabell
Mrs. Elizabeth Cabell
Representative Raymond Roberts

National Press Pool Car
Merriman Smith, UPI
Malcolm Kilduff
Robert Baskin, DMN
Jack Bell, AP
Bob Clark, ABC

Camera Car One
John Hofan, NBC
Dave Wiegman Jr., NBC
Thomas Craven, CBS
Cleveland Ryan
Thomas Atkins, USN

Camera Car Two
Clint Grant, DMN
Frank Cancallare, UPI
Cecil Stoughton, White House photographer
Arthur Rickerby, *Life Magazine*
Henry Burroughs, AP

Camera Car Three
James Underwood, KRLD
Tom Dillard, DMN
James Darnell
Malcolm Couch, WFAA
Robert Jackson, DTH

DPD Motorcycles
H. B. McLain
Marrion Baker

Congressional Car One
Representative George Mahon
Representative Walter Rogers
Representative Homer Thornberry
Lawrence O'Brien

Congressional Car Two
Representative Albert Thomas
Representative Jack Brooks
Representative Lindy Beckworth
Representative Olin Teague
Representative Jim Wright

Congressional Car Three
Representative John Young
Representative Henry Gonzalez
State Representative William Pateman

VIP Car
General Chester Clifton, USA
General Godfrey McHugh, USAF
Julian Reed

DPD Motorcycles
J. W. Courson
Clyde Haygood
Sergeant R. Smart
Bobby Joe Dale

US Secret Service Code Names: JFK Presidency

ACROBAT
Andrews Air Force Base

ANGEL
Air Force One

CACTUS
Camp David

CORK
FBI Headquarters

CROWN
White House Executive Mansion

DAGGER
SA Rufus Youngblood

DANDY
SA Lem Johns

DAPPER
SA John O'Leary

DASHER
SA Tom Wells

DAYLIGHT
SA Jerry Kivett

DAZZLE
SA Clint Hill

DEACON
SA Floyd Boring

DEBUT
SA Paul Landis

DIGEST
SA Roy Kellerman

DOMINO
SS Chief, James Rowley

DRAGON
SA John Campion

DRESSER
SA Bob Foster

DRUMMER
SA Lynn Meredith

DUPLEX
SA Gerald Behn

DUSTY
SA Emory Roberts

FREEDOM
Secretary of State Dean Rusk

LACE
Jacqueline Kennedy

LANCER
President John F. Kennedy

LARK
John F. Kennedy Jr.

LYRIC
Caroline Kennedy

MARKET
Admiral George Burkley, JFK's Physician

TIGER
Colonel James Swindal, *Air Force One* Pilot

TOURIST
Major William Brown, Military Aide

VARSITY
Vice Presidential Follow-up Car

VELVET
Lynda Bird Johnson

VENUS
Lucy Baines Johnson

VICTORIA
Lady Bird Johnson

VOLUNTEER
Vice President Lyndon Johnson

WAND
Kenneth O'Donnell

WARRIOR
Malcolm Kilduff

WATCHMAN
General Chester Clifton, JFK's Military Aide

WAYSIDE
Pierre Salinger

WILLOW
Evelyn Lincoln, JFK's Personal Secretary

WING
General Godfrey McHugh, JFK'S Military Aide

WITNESS
Captain Tazewell Shepard JFK's Naval Aide

APPENDIX III

DID YOU KNOW?

1. John F. Kennedy was the youngest man (forty-three) ever elected to the presidency. The youngest serving president was Theodore Roosevelt (forty-two).

2. As a child, Kennedy suffered from a plethora of maladies including chicken pox, scarlet fever, whooping cough, and the measles.

3. Prior to his assassination, JFK was administered the last rites on four separate occasions.

4. Before Jacqueline Bouvier and John F. Kennedy's wedding mass, a special blessing from Pope Pius XII was read.

5. Although the bride desired a small wedding, her future father-in-law, Joseph Kennedy Sr., insisted on a lavish affair inviting 1,200 guests to the reception.

6. In 1958, future TV host Larry King was involved in a traffic accident with then-Senator Kennedy in Palm Beach, Florida.

7. The melody from Frank Sinatra's 1959 recording of "High Hopes" was the basis for JFK's presidential campaign song. The lyrics for both versions were written by Oscar-winning songwriter Sammy Cahn.

8. Kennedy's one-minute presidential campaign commercial mentioned his name twenty-seven times.

9. On November 8, 1960, Senator John F. Kennedy was elected president by winning fewer states, but more electoral votes than Vice President Richard Nixon.

10. JFK was the first person born in the twentieth century to become president.

11. Prior to Kennedy, only five US presidents had graduated from Harvard.

12. JFK was the only US president to be awarded the Pulitzer Prize and the Presidential Medal of Freedom.

13. Kennedy was the last president to wear a top hat at his inauguration.

14. On March 22, 1961, President Kennedy signed his first bill into law. Designated Public Law 87-3, it restored the military rank of General of the Army to former President Dwight Eisenhower.

15. With an estimated wealth of $100 million, JFK donated his entire presidential salary to charity. Recipients included the Boy Scouts of America, the Cuban Families Committee, and the United Negro College Fund.

16. An avid reader, Kennedy's favorite books were *Marlborough: His Life and Times*, *The Guns of August*, *The Emergence of Lincoln*, and *Pilgrim's Way*.

17. In total, JFK authored three books. The last, *A Nation of Immigrants*, was published posthumously in 1964.

18. Country music star Jimmy Dean scored a 1962 hit with "PT-109" about the wartime exploits of Lieutenant John F. Kennedy. It charted at No. 3 on the US *Billboard* Hot Country Singles and No. 8 on the US *Billboard* Hot 100. Other military-oriented songs released in the 1960's included Johnny Horton's "Sink the Bismarck" and Sergeant Barry Sadler's "The Ballad of the Green Berets."

19. Impressionist Vaughn Meader skyrocketed to fame with an uncanny impersonation of JFK. His Grammy-winning album *The First Family* stayed at No. 1 on the *Billboard* 200 for twelve weeks, selling an astounding seven million copies.

20. During the second year of his presidency, Kennedy had a tape-recording system installed in the Oval Office. Following his death, it was disconnected.

21. JFK signed his last bill into law on October 31, 1963. Designated Public Law 88-164, the Mental Retardation and Community Mental Health Centers Construction Act provided funding for outpatient psychiatric facilities and the development of more effective psychotropic medications.

22. On the day of his assassination, President Kennedy wore a Brooks Brothers charcoal suit and white striped shirt with a dark-blue Christian Dior necktie.

23. *Air Force One*, designated Special Air Mission (SAM) 26000, was the Boeing 707 that carried Kennedy to Dallas and later returned his body to Washington, DC. Custom built in 1962, it served a total of eight presidents. Retired in 1998, it is on permanent display at the National Museum of the US Air Force in Dayton, Ohio.

24. For the Texas trip, a US Air Force C-123 cargo plane was used to transport JFK's limousine. A modified 1961 Lincoln Continental, it was outfitted with rear bumper steps, a two-way communication system, auxiliary jump seats, and flashing red lights and siren. Following the assassination, it was delivered to Hess & Eisenhardt in Cincinnati, Ohio for upgrades, including bulletproof glass and a hard-top roof. It remained in service until 1977. Currently, it is on display at the Henry Ford Museum in Dearborn, Michigan.

25. The presidential parade car was central to the tragic events on November 22, 1963, but these automobiles also played important roles:

- **1961 Lincoln Continental convertible**—On loan from Golightly Auto Sales, it moved JFK and the first lady from a morning event in Fort Worth, Texas, to Carswell Air Force Base for the brief flight to Dallas. In 2020, the limousine sold at auction for $375,000.

- **1962 Checker Marathon taxicab**—Registration No. RI-2-6161, it transported Lee Harvey Oswald from downtown Dallas to his rooming house following the assassination. In 1979, it was donated by the Checker Motor Corporation to the Pate Museum in Fort Worth. In 2010, it was sold at auction for $35,750. The vehicle is currently on display at Historic Auto Attractions in Roscoe, Illinois.

- **1963 Pontiac Bonneville ambulance**—Designated US Navy 94-49196, it received JFK's body at Andrews Air Force Base and, following the autopsy, carried his remains to the White House. Ownership of the ambulance was transferred from the US Navy to the John F. Kennedy Presidential Library and Museum in 1980. The vehicle was eventually destroyed at a Boston junkyard in 1986. A reasonable facsimile was sold at auction in 2011 for $132,000.

- **1964 Cadillac hearse**—License number WC 609, it transferred the slain president from Parkland Hospital back to *Air Force One*. Produced by the Miller-Meteor Company, the funeral coach was sold at a Barrett-Jackson auction in 2012 for $160,000. The vehicle is currently on display at the Graham County Auto and Arts Museum in Hill City, Kansas.

26. All three TV networks (ABC, CBS, and NBC) covered the assassination for four continuous days.

27. JFK's assassination was the longest uninterrupted news story on TV until the September 11, 2001 terrorist attacks.

28. President Kennedy's maternal grandmother was never told that her grandson had been assassinated. She died in 1964 at the age of ninety-eight.

29. Among the items placed in the slain president's casket were gold cuff links, a PT-109 tie clip, and silver rosary beads.

30. The horse-drawn caisson that carried JFK's body had also been used for the funerals of Abraham Lincoln and FDR.

31. Members of the burial detail represented all five branches of the US military. They included:

- Lieutenant Samuel R. Bird (USA)
- Yeoman George A. Barnum (USCG)
- Seaman Larry B. Smith (USN)
- Lance Corporal Jerry J. Diamond (USMC)
- Seaman Hubert Clark (USN)
- Lance Corporal Timothy F. Cheeks (USMC)
- Sergeant Richard E. Gaudreau (USAF)
- Corporal Douglas A. Mayfield (USA)
- Sergeant James L. Felder (USA)

32. More than 250,000 mourners filed past the late president's flag-draped coffin in the Capitol Rotunda.

33. Five US military bands provided the solemn music at JFK's funeral: the Coast Guard Academy Band, the Marine Band, the Navy Band, the Air Force Band, and the Army Band. Musical selections included "Hail to the Chief," "Our Fallen Heroes," "America the Beautiful," "Holy God, We Praise Thy Name," and "Eternal Father, Strong to Save."

34. Some eight hundred thousand people lined Pennsylvania Avenue in Washington, DC, to pay their respects to President Kennedy.

35. According to the Nielsen organization, an estimated 93 percent of American TVs were turned on for JFK's funeral.

36. In Sioux City, Iowa, a man named Vaschia Michael Bohan was watching the funeral on TV when his stepfather entered the room and made a disparaging remark about JFK. Angered by what he said, Bohan picked up a pair of scissors and stabbed his stepfather to death. Bohan was charged with manslaughter and pled guilty but received a suspended sentence and a $1,000 fine. The charitable judge justified his decision by stating that the entire nation was under a great emotional strain.

37. The eternal flame on JFK's grave was lighted by Jacqueline Kennedy on November 25, 1963. It has only been extinguished twice.

38. Kennedy was the second US president buried in Arlington Cemetery. The first was William Howard Taft.

39. The only Kennedy brother not buried at Arlington is Joseph Kennedy Jr. A naval aviator during World War II, he was killed while on a top-secret mission. His remains were never recovered.

40. *Variety*, the Hollywood trade publication, estimated that the JFK assassination cost the TV and film industries $40 million.

41. In honor of President Kennedy's commitment to the US space program, Cape Canaveral was renamed Cape Kennedy by Executive Order 11129 on November 29, 1963. Bowing to public pressure, the Florida state legislature restored the name to Cape Canaveral in 1973.

42. The solid bronze Handley Britannia casket that bore JFK's remains from Dallas to Bethesda was stored at the National Archives until the winter of 1966, when it was filled with three eighty-pound sandbags, moved to Andrews Air Force Base, flown in a C-130 transport plane one hundred miles off the coast of Delaware, and unceremoniously dropped in the Atlantic Ocean.

43. Beginning in the mid-1960s, a list of Lincoln / Kennedy coincidences began to appear in the media. While some have no basis in fact, others are historically accurate. For example:

- Lincoln was elected to the House of Representatives in 1846, Kennedy in 1946.
- Lincoln was elected to the presidency in 1860, Kennedy in 1960.
- Both presidents had the same number of vowels and consonants in the same sequence in their last names.
- Lincoln and Kennedy were in their thirties when they married women in their twenties.
- Both presidents had four children.
- Both presidents lost a child while in the White House.
- Both presidents were killed on a Friday.
- Both presidents were shot in the back of the head.
- Both first ladies were present when their husbands were assassinated.
- Both assassins committed their crimes at locations where they were employed.
- Both assassins were killed before standing trial.
- Both assassins were known by their first, middle, and last names.
- Both assassins were in their twenties.

- John Wilkes Booth shot Lincoln in a theatre, and Lee Harvey Oswald was captured in a theatre.
- The names John Wilkes Booth and Lee Harvey Oswald each contain fifteen letters.
- Lincoln was assassinated in Ford's Theatre, and Kennedy was assassinated while riding in a Lincoln, an automobile produced by the Ford Motor Company.
- Lincoln and Kennedy were succeeded by men named Johnson.
- Andrew Johnson was born in 1808, and Lyndon Johnson was born in 1908.
- Both Johnsons had thirteen letters in their names.
- Both Johnsons were from the South. Andrew was from South Carolina, and Lyndon was from Texas.

44. Acting on two of JFK's legislative initiatives, President Lyndon Johnson signed into law the landmark Civil Rights Act of 1964 and the Voting Rights Act of 1965.

45. The death of President John F. Kennedy and the issue of presidential succession led to the ratification of the Twenty-Fifth Amendment on February 10, 1967.

46. One of the enduring images from that day in Dallas is the Hertz-Rent-A-Car sign that sat atop the Texas School Book Depository. The enamel-and-metal billboard registered 12:30 p.m. as the president's limousine traveled down Elm Street and into history. In 1979, it was removed and is the property of the Sixth Floor Museum at Dealey Plaza.

47. The Texas School Book Depository sign located above the building's Elm Street entrance was also taken down in the 1970s. It was later restored and added to the Sixth Floor Museum collection in 1983.

48. In April 1931, a small cinema opened in the Oak Cliff section of Dallas called the Texas Theater. On November 22, 1963, it gained worldwide

notoriety as the movie house where Lee Harvey Oswald was captured. Closed by United Artists in 1989, the building narrowly missed demolition in 1993 and was nearly destroyed by a devastating fire two years later. However, In September 2021, through the combined efforts of the Oak Cliff Foundation and the city of Dallas, the theater was completely refurbished and reopened to the public. Because of its historical significance, it was designated a Dallas Landmark in 2001 and was listed in the National Register of Historic Places in 2003.

49. Governor John Connally survived his life-threatening wounds and remained in office until 1969. He later served in the Nixon administration as secretary of the treasury. Although the Warren Commission concluded that both JFK and Connally were wounded by the same bullet, Connally consistently maintained that he was struck by a separate bullet. He died in 1993 at the age of seventy-six.

50. In 1999, an arbitration panel awarded the heirs of Abraham Zapruder a staggering $16 million for his original twenty-six-second film. That same year, the family donated the film's copyright to the Sixth Floor Museum.

ABBREVIATIONS AND ACRONYMS

ABC: American Broadcasting Company
AP: Associated Press
ASAIC: Assistant special agent-in-charge
CBS: Columbia Broadcasting System
CIA: Central Intelligence Agency
DEA: Drug Enforcement Administration
DMN: *Dallas Morning News*
DPD: Dallas Police Department
DTH: *Dallas Times Herald*
FBI: Federal Bureau of Investigation
HSCA: House Select Committee on Assassinations
KGB: Committee for State Security
KRLD: AM radio station in Dallas, Texas
NBC: National Broadcasting Company
NSA: National Security Agency
NSC: National Security Council
PBS: Public Broadcasting Service
PT: Patrol Torpedo
ROTC: Reserve Officers' Training Corps
SA: Special agent
TSHP: Texas State Highway Patrol
UPI: United Press International
US: United States
USA: United States Army

USAF: United States Air Force
USCG: United States Coast Guard
USMC: United States Marine Corps
USN: United States Navy
WC: Warren Commission
WFAA: ABC-affiliated TV station in Dallas, Texas

About the Author

William E. Scott is an award-winning educator who earned his BA in American History from West Chester University and graduate degrees from Villanova University and American Military University. The author of *November 22, 1963: A Reference Guide to the JFK Assassination*, he currently resides in Springfield, Pennsylvania with his wife, Diane.

ENDNOTES

INTRODUCTION

1 Andrew Cohen, "How to Watch the Kennedy Assassination Coverage as It Happened," *The Atlantic, November* 18, 2013, https://www.theatlantic.com/national/archive/2012/11/how-to-watch-the-kennedy-assassination-coverage-as-it-happened/281568.

2 *Frontline:Who Was Lee Harvey Oswald?*, produced by William Cran and Ben Loeterman, InVision Productions, 2013, DVD.

CHAPTER ONE: US PRESIDENTIAL ASSASSINATIONS AND ATTEMPTED ASSASSINATIONS

3 Michael W. Kauffman, *American Brutus: John Wilkes Booth and the Lincoln Conspiracies* (New York: Random House, 2004), 7, 14.

4 Terry Alford, *Fortune's Fool: The Life of John Wilkes Booth* (New York: Oxford University Press, 2015), 313.

5 Margaret Leech and Harry J. Brown, *The Garfield Orbit: The Life of President James Garfield* (New York: Harper & Row, 1978), 244.

6 Ira Rutkow, *James A. Garfield* (New York: Times Books, 2006), 83.

7 Jay Bellamy, "A Stalwart of Stalwarts: Garfield's Assassin Sees Deed as a Special Duty," *Prologue Magazine,* Fall 2016, https://www.archives.gov/publications/prologue/2016/fall/ quiteau

8 Robert W. Merry, *President McKinley: Architect of the American Century* (New York: Simon & Schuster, 2017), 480.

CHAPTER TWO: JOHN F. KENNEDY

9 Robert Dallek, *An Unfinished Life: John F. Kennedy, 1917–1963* (Boston: Little, Brown and Company), 693.

10 Gerald Posner, *Case Closed* (New York: Random House, 1993), 233.

11 William Manchester, *The Death of a President* (New York: Back Bay Books, 2013), 218.

CHAPTER THREE: LEE HARVEY OSWALD

12 Manchester, *Death*, 284.

13 *Report of the President's Commission on the Assassination of President John F. Kennedy* (Washington, DC: US Government Printing Office, 1964), 423.

14 Vincent Bugliosi, *Reclaiming History: The Assassination of President John F. Kennedy* (New York: W. W. Norton & Company, 2007), 273.

CHAPTER FOUR: JACK RUBY

15 Gary Cartwright, "Who Was Jack Ruby?" *Texas Monthly*, November 1, 1975, https://www.texasmonthly.com/news-politics/who-was-jack-ruby.

16 Philip Shenon, *A Cruel and Shocking Act: The Secret History of the Kennedy Assassination* (New York: Henry Holt and Company, 2013), 190.

17 Dan Abrams and David Fisher, *Kennedy's Avenger: Assassination, Conspiracy, and the Forgotten Trial of Jack Ruby* (New York: Hanover Square Press, 2021), 27.

18 Manchester, *Death*, 524.

19 Abrams and Fisher, *Kennedy's Avenger*, 67.

CHAPTER FIVE: THE WARREN COMMISSION

20 D. J. Herda, *Earl Warren: A Life of Truth and Justice* (Guilford, CT: Prometheus Books, 2019), 214.

21 President's Commission on the Assassination of President John F. Kennedy, *Hearings Before the President's Commission on the Assassination of President Kennedy*, vol. 2 (Washington, DC: US Government Printing Office, 1964), 73.

22 Posner, *Case Closed*, 13.

23 President's Commission, *Hearings*, vol. 1, 119.

24 President's Commission, *Hearings*, vol. 3, 194.

25 "Editorial: The Warren Commission Report," *The New York Times*, September 28, 1964, 28.

26 Loudon Wainwright, "The View: The Book for All to Read," *Life Magazine*, October 16, 1964, 35.

CHAPTER SIX: THE GARRISON INVESTIGATION AND OTHER CONSPIRACIES

27 Tom Flynn, "Who Really Killed JFK? Experts Pick the Wildest Conspiracy Theories," *The Daily Beast*, November 20, 2013, https://www.thedailybeast.com/who-really-killed-jfk-experts-pick-the- wildest-conspiracy-theories?ref=scroll.

28 Byron Tau, "Kerry Won't Talk about Kennedy Conspiracy," *Politico*, November 10, 2013, https://www.politico.com/blogs/politico-now/2013/11/kerry-wont-talk-about-kennedy-conspiracy-177167.

29 Philip Shenon, "The Spy Chief Who Lied," *Politico Magazine*, October 6, 2015, https://www.politico.com/magazine/story/2015/10/jfk-assassination-john-mccone-warren- commission-cia-213197.

30 Dan Spinelli, "Trump Revives Rumor Linking Cruz's Father to JFK Assassination," *Politico*, July 22, 2016, https://www.politico.com/story/2016-07/trump-ted-cruz-jfk-assassination-226020.

CHAPTER SEVEN: IN THEIR OWN WORDS

31 Larry J. Sabato, *The Kennedy Half-Century* (New York: Bloomsbury, 2013), 12.

32 Sabato, *Kennedy Half-Century*, 12.

33 Cyril Wecht and Dawna Kaufmann, *The JFK Assassination Dissected: An Analysis by Forensic Pathologist Cyril Wecht* (Jefferson, NC: Exposit, 2022), 12.

34 Dean R. Owen, *November 22, 1963: Reflections on the Life, Assassination, and Legacy of John F. Kennedy* (New York: Skyhorse Publishing, 2013), 126.

35 President's Commission, *Hearings*, vol. 7, 473.

36 Jon Herskovitz, "How the JFK Assassination Transformed Media Coverage," *Reuters*, November 21, 2013, https://www.reuters.com/article/us-usa-jfk-media-idUSBRE9AK11N 20131121.

37 Lisa Maria Garza, et al., "Factbox: Quotes on 50th Anniversary of Kennedy's Assassination," *Reuters*, November 22, 2013, https://www.reuters.com/article/ususa-jfk-factbox-idUSBRE9AL14L20131122.

38 President's Commission, *Hearings*, vol. 6, 43.

39 Mark North, *Act of Treason* (New York: Skyhorse Publishing, 2011), 386.

40 Garza et al., "Factbox."

41 North, *Act*, 379.

42 Gerald Blaine, *The Kennedy Detail: JFK's Secret Service Agents Break Their Silence* (New York: Gallery Books, 2010), 224.

43 Garza et al., "Factbox."

44 Garza et al., "Factbox."

45 Owen, *November 22, 1963*, 149.

46 Garza et al., "Factbox."

47 David Talbot, *Brothers: The Hidden History of the Kennedy Years* (New York: Free Press, 2007), 277.

48 Joan Mellen, *A Farewell to Justice: Jim Garrison, JFK's Assassination, and the Case That Should Have Changed History* (Lincoln, NE: Potomac Books, 2007), 357.

49 President's Commission, *Hearings*, vol. 6, 296.

50 Owen, *November 22, 1963*, 179.

51 Alan Brinkley, *John F. Kennedy: The American President's Series: The 35th President, 1961–1963*, (New York: Times Books, 2012), 156.

52 President's Commission, *Hearings*, vol. 10, 353.

53 Garza et al., "Factbox."

54 Talbot, *Brothers*, 12.

55 Talbot, *Brothers*, 23.

56 Owen, *November 22, 1963*, 109.

57 Michael O'Brien, *John F. Kennedy: A Biography* (New York: Thomas Dunne Books, 2005), 903.

58 President's Commission, *Hearings*, vol. 6, 298–99.

59 President's Commission, *Hearings*, vol. 9, 444.

60 Abrams and Fisher, *Kennedy's Avenger*, 17.

61 Owen, *November 22, 1963*, 193.

62 Garza et al., "Factbox."

63 Alexandra Zapruder, *Twenty-Six Seconds: A Personal History of the Zapruder Film* (New York: Twelve, 2016), 36.

64 Mellen, *Farewell*, 264.

65 Steven M. Gillon, *The Kennedy Assassination: 24 Hours After: Lyndon B. Johnson's Pivotal First Day as President* (New York: Basic Press, 2009), 26.

66 President's Commission, *Hearings*, vol., 3, 354.

67 President's Commission, *Hearings*, vol. 6, 53.

68 Owen, *November 22, 1963*, 133.

69 President's Commission, *Hearings*, vol. 6, 237

70 President's Commission, *Hearings*, vol. 3, 211.

71 Shenon, *A Cruel and Shocking Act*, 526.

72 President's Commission, *Hearings*, vol. 6, 157.

73 President's Commission, *Hearings*, vol. 6, 163.

74 President's Commission, *Hearings*, vol. 2, 193.

75 President's Commission, *Hearings*, vol. 1, 463.

76 President's Commission, *Hearings*, vol. 7, 518.

77 President's Commission, *Hearings*, vol. 6, 338.

78 Abrams and Fisher, *Kennedy's Avenger*, 12.

79 Abrams and Fisher, *Kennedy's Avenger*, 81.

80 Blaine, *Kennedy Detail*, 211.

81 President's Commission, *Hearings*, vol. 12, 399.

82 Blaine, *Kennedy Detail*, 214.

83 Mellen, *Farewell*, 3.

84   President's Commission, *Hearings*, vol. 15, 74.

85   President's Commission, *Hearings*, vol. 6, 234.

86   President's Commission, *Hearings* vol. 7, 478

87   Owen, *November 22, 1963*, 34–35.

88   President's Commission, *Hearings*, vol. 6, 448.

89   Gus Russo and Harry Moses, eds., *Where Were You? America Remembers the JFK Assassination* (Guilford, CT: Lyons Press, 2013), 3.

90   President's Commission, *Hearings*, vol. 7, 478.

91   Russo and Moses, *Where Were You?*, 22.

92   President's Commission, *Hearings*, vol. 12, 39.

93   President's Commission, *Hearings*, vol. 1, 207.

94   Gillon, *Kennedy Assassination*, 48.

95   Russo and Moses, *Where Were You?*, 33.

96   Russo and Moses, *Where Were You?*, 248.

97   Shenon, *A Cruel and Shocking Act*, 60.

98   Shenon, *A Cruel and Shocking Act*, 84.

99   Owen, *November 22, 1963*, 312.

100   Harold Weisberg, *Whitewash IV* (New York: Skyhorse Publishing, 2013), 21.

101   Shenon, *A Cruel and Shocking Act*, 82.

102   President's Commission, *Hearings*, vol. 6, 364–65.

103   President's Commission, *Hearings*, vol. 6, 143.

104   President's Commission, *Hearings*, vol. 6, 136.

105   President's Commission, *Hearings*, vol. 6, 145.

106   Russo and Moses, *Where Were You?*, 13.

107   President's Commission, *Hearings*, vol. 2, 204.

108   President's Commission, *Hearings*, vol. 4, 356

109   *Frontline*.

110   Brinkley, *John F. Kennedy*, 154.

111   Wecht and Kaufmann, *JFK Assassination Dissected*, 13.

112   Wecht and Kaufmann, *JFK Assassination Dissected*, 13.

113   Gillon, *Kennedy Assassination*, 81.

114   Gillon, *Kennedy Assassination*, 93.

115   Gillon, *Kennedy Assassination*, 51.

116   Russo and Moses, *Where Were You?*, 256.

117   David R. Wrone, *The Zapruder Film: Reframing JFK's Assassination* (Lawrence, KS: University Press of Kansas, 2003), 247.

118   Russo and Moses, *Where Were You?*, 331.

119   President's Commission, *Hearings*, vol. 6, 330.

120   President's Commission, *Hearings*, vol. 3, 292.

121   President's Commission, *Hearings*, vol. 10, 227.

122   President's Commission, *Hearings*, vol. 7, 440.

123   President's Commission, *Hearings*, vol. 7, 112.

124   President's Commission, *Hearings*, vol. 2, 148–49.

125   President's Commission, *Hearings*, vol. 6, 169.

126   Blaine, *Kennedy Detail*, 212.

127   Sabato, *Kennedy Half-Century*, 187.

128   Owen, *November 22, 1963*, 176.

129   Jim Bishop, *The Day Kennedy Was Shot* (New York: Harper Perennial, 2013), xi.

130   Cohen, "How to Watch."

CHAPTER EIGHT: LITERATURE

131   David R. Wrone, Review of *Case Closed* by Gerald Posner, *The Journal of Southern History* 61, no. 1 (1995), 186–88.

132   Edwin Shrake, *Strange Peaches* (Houston, TX: John M. Harding Publishing Company, 2007), front cover.

133   James W. Douglass, *JFK and the Unspeakable: Why He Died and Why It Matters* (New York: Touchstone, 2010), back cover.

134   Kevin James Shay, *Death of the Rising Sun: A Search for Truth in the JFK Assassination* (Washington, DC: Random Publishers, 2017), 16.

135   Sabato, *Kennedy Half-Century*, 1.

136   Larry M. Sturdivan, *The JFK Myths: A Scientific Investigation of the Kennedy Assassination* (St. Paul, MN, 2005), back cover.

137   Blaine, *Kennedy Detail*, i.

CHAPTER NINE: DOCUMENTARIES, FILMS, AND TV PROGRAMS

138   *The JFK Assassination: The Jim Garrison Tapes*, 96 minutes, produced by Sarita Barbour, et al., (Live Home Video, 1992), VHS, https://www.imdb.com.

139   *Interview with the Assassin*, 88 minutes, directed by Neil Burger (Showtime Entertainment, 2003), DVD.

140   Brady Langmann, "*The Irishman* Makes a Subtle Reference to the Mafia's Suspected Involvement in JFK's Assassination," *Esquire*, October 1, 2019, https://www.esquire.com /entertainment/movies/a29322953/ the-irishman-jfk-assassination-mob-mafia-theory-frank-sheeran-true-story.

141   Tom Shales, "The (Tasteless) Trial of Oswald," *The Washington Post*, September 30, 1977, C8.

142   *Love Field*, 105 minutes, directed by Jonathan Kaplan (MGM, 2001), DVD, https://www.imdb.com.

143   *The Kennedys,* 353 minutes, produced by John Cassar, et al. (Lionsgate, 2011), DVD, https://www.imdb.com.

144   *Fatal Deception: Mrs. Lee Harvey Oswald*, 91 minutes, produced by Paul Pompian, (Warner Archives Collection, 2013), DVD.

145   *11.22.63*, 450 minutes, produced by John David Coles, et al. (Warner Brothers, 2016), DVD, https//www.imdb.com.

146   *Ruby and Oswald*, 100 minutes, produced by Paul Freeman (Fremantle Media, 2007), DVD, https//www.imdb.com.

147   *In the Line of Fire,* 129 minutes, directed by Wolfgang Peterson (Sony Pictures Home Entertainment, 2001), DVD.

148   *JFK*, 189 minutes, directed by Oliver Stone (Warner Home Video, 1997), DVD, https:// www.imdb.com.

149   *Killing Kennedy*, 87 minutes, produced by Larry Rapaport (Twentieth Century Home Entertainment, 2014), DVD.

150   *Ruby*, 100 minutes, directed by John MacKenzie (Sony Pictures Home Entertainment, 2003), DVD, https://www.imdb.com.

151   *Interview with the Assassin*, https://www.imdb.com.

152   *Executive Action,* 91 minutes, directed by David Miller (Warner Home Video, 2007), DVD.

153   *Parkland,* 94 minutes, directed by Peter Landesman (Exclusive Media, 2013), DVD, https://www.imdb.com.

CHAPTER TEN: 1963: THE YEAR IN REVIEW

154   Richard Reeves, *President Kennedy: Profile of Power* (New York: Simon & Schuster, 1993), 515.

BIBLIOGRAPHY

GOVERNMENT PUBLICATIONS

President's Commission on the Assassination of President John F. Kennedy. *Hearings Before the President's Commission on the Assassination of President Kennedy.* 26 vols. Washington, DC: US Government Printing Office, 1964.

_____. *Report of the President's Commission on the Assassination of President John F. Kennedy.* Washington, DC: US Government Printing Office, 1964.

United States House of Representatives Select Committee on Assassinations. *Report of the Select Committee on Assassinations of the U.S. House of Representatives,* Washington, DC: US Government Printing Office, 1979.

BOOKS

Abrams, Dan, and David Fisher. *Kennedy's Avenger: Assassination, Conspiracy, and the Forgotten Trial of Jack Ruby.* New York: Hanover Square Press, 2021.

Adelson, Alan. *The Ruby-Oswald Affair: Reflection by Alan Adelson.* Seattle, WA: Robert Ruby, 1988.

Alford, Terry. *Fortune's Fool: The Life of John Wilkes Booth.* New York: New Oxford Press, 2015.

Axlerod, Alan. *Lost Destiny: Joe Kennedy Jr. and the Doomed WWII Mission to Save London.* New York: St. Martin's Press, 2015.

Bishop. Jim. *The Day Kennedy Was Shot.* New York: Harper Perennial, 2013.

Blaine, Gerald. *The Kennedy Detail: JFK's Secret Service Agents Break Their Silence.* New York: Gallery Books, 2010.

Bremer, Arthur H. *An Assassin's Diary.* New York: Harper's Magazine Press, 1973.

Brinkley, Alan. *John F. Kennedy: The American President's Series: The 35th President, 1961–1963.* New York: Times Books, 2012.

Bugliosi, Vincent. *Reclaiming History: The Assassination of President John F. Kennedy.* New York: W. W. Norton & Company, 2007.

Dallek, Robert. *An Unfinished Life: John F. Kennedy, 1917–1963.* Boston, MA: Little, Brown and Company, 2003.

Davis, John H. *Mafia Kingfish.* New York: McGraw-Hill, 1989.

DeLillo, Don. *Libra.* New York: Viking Press, 1988.

Donald, David Herbert. *Lincoln.* New York: Simon & Schuster, 1995.

Douglass, James W. *JFK and the Unspeakable: Why He Died and Why It Matters.* New York: Touchstone, 2010.

Doyle, William. *PT 109: An American Epic of War, Survival, and the Destiny of John F. Kennedy.* New York: William Morrow, 2015.

Ellroy, James. *American Tabloid.* New York: Alfred E. Knopf, 1995.

Epstein, Edward Jay. *Legend: The Secret World of Lee Harvey Oswald.* New York: Reader's Digest Press, 1978.

_____. *Sixty Versions of the Kennedy Assassination: A Primer on Conspiracy Theories.* Scotts Valley, CA: CreateSpace, 2013.

Gillon, Steven M. *The Kennedy Assassination: 24 Hours After: Lyndon B. Johnson's Pivotal First Day as President.* New York: Basic Books, 2009.

Herda, D. J. *Earl Warren: A Life of Truth and Justice.* Guilford, CT: Prometheus Books, 2019.

Hinckle, Warren, and William Turner. *Deadly Secrets.* New York: Basic Books, 1993.

Kauffman, Michael W. *American Brutus: John Wilkes Booth and the Lincoln Conspiracies.* New York: Random House, 2004.

Kurtz, Michael. *Crime of the Century: The Kennedy Assassination from a Historian's Perspective.* Knoxville, TN: University of Tennessee Press, 2013.

Leech, Margaret, and Harry J. Brown, *The Garfield Orbit: The Life of President James Garfield.* New York: Harper & Row, 1978.

Loken, John. *Oswald's Trigger Films.* Ann Arbor, MI: Falcon Books, 2000.

Mailer, Norman. *Oswald's Tale: An American Mystery.* New York: Random House, 1995.

Manchester, William. *The Death of a President*. New York: Back Bay Books, 2013.

McKnight, Gerald D. *Breach of Trust: How the Warren Commission Failed the Nation and Why*. Lawrence, KS: University Press of Kansas, 2005.

Mellen, Joan. *A Farewell to Justice: Jim Garrison, JFK's Assassination, and the Case That Should Have Changed History*. Lincoln, NE: Potomac Books, 2007.

_____. *Jim Garrison: His Life and Times—The Early Years*. Southlake, TX: JFK Lancer Production & Publications, 2008.

Meltzer, Brad, and Josh Mensch. *The Lincoln Conspiracy: The Secret Plot to Kill America's 16th President—And Why It Failed*. New York: Flatiron Press, 2020.

Merry, Robert W. *President McKinley: Architect of the American Century*. New York: Simon & Schuster, 2017.

North, Mark. *Act of Treason*. New York: Skyhorse Publishing, 2011.

Noyes, Peter. *Legacy of Doubt*. New York: Pinnacle Books, 1973.

O'Brien, Michael. *John F. Kennedy: A Biography*. New York: Thomas Dunne Books, 2005.

O'Donnell, Kenneth P., and David F. Powers. *"Johnny, We Hardly Knew Ye."* Boston, MA: Little, Brown and Company, 1972.

Owen, Dean R. *November 22, 1963: Reflections on the Life, Assassination, and Legacy of John F. Kennedy*. New York: Skyhorse Publishing, 2013.

Posner, Gerald. *Case Closed*. New York: Random House, 1993.

Reeves, Richard. *President Kennedy: Profile of Power*. New York: Simon & Schuster, 1993.

Russo, Gus, and Harry Moses, eds. *Where Were You? America Remembers the JFK Assassination*. Guilford, CT: Lyons Press, 2013.

Rutkow, Ira. *James A. Garfield*. New York: Times Books, 2006.

Sabato, Larry J. *The Kennedy Half-Century*. New York: Bloomsbury, 2013.

Shay, Kevin James. *Death of the Rising Sun: A Search for Truth in the JFK Assassination*. Washington, DC: Random Publishers, 2017.

Shenon, Philip. *A Cruel and Shocking Act: The Secret History of the Kennedy Assassination*. New York: Henry Holt and Company, 2013.

Shrake, Edwin. *Strange Peaches*. Houston, TX: John M. Harding Publishing Company, 2007.

Sturdivan, Larry M. *The JFK Myths: A Scientific Investigation of the Kennedy Assassination*, St. Paul, MN, 2005.

Talbot, David. *Brothers: The Hidden History of the Kennedy Years*. New York: Free Press, 2007.

Trask, Richard B. *Pictures of the Pain: Photography and the Assassination of President Kennedy*. Danvers, MA: Yeoman Press, 1994.

Wecht, Cyril, and Dawna Kaufmann. *The JFK Assassination Dissected: An Analysis by Forensic Pathologist Cyril Wecht*. Jefferson, NC: Exposit, 2022.

Weisberg, Harold. *Case Open*. New York: Carroll & Graf Publishers, 1994.

_____. *Whitewash IV.* New York: Skyhorse Publishing, 2013.

Willens, Howard. *History Will Prove Us Right: Inside the Warren Commission Report on the Assassination of John F. Kennedy*. New York: Abrams Press, 2013.

Wills, Gary, and Ovid Demaris. *Jack Ruby*. Boston, MA: DaCapo Press, 1994.

Wrone, David R. *The Zapruder Film: Reframing JFK's Assassination*. Lawrence, KS: University Press of Kansas, 2003.

Yanoff, Stephen G. *Gone Before Glory: The Life and Tragic Death of William McKinley*. Bloomington, IN: AuthorHouse, 2021.

Zapruder, Alexandra. *Twenty-Six Seconds: A Personal History of the Zapruder Film*. New York: Twelve, 2016.

PERIODICALS

Shales, Tom. "The (Tasteless) Trial of Oswald." *The Washington Post*. September 30, 1977, C8.

Wainwright, Loudon. "The View: The Book for All to Read." *Life Magazine*. October 16, 1964, 35.

The New York Times. "Editorial: The Warren Commission Report." September 28, 1964, 28.

JOURNALS

Wrone, David R. [Review of *Case Closed* by Gerald Posner]. *The Journal of Southern History* 61, no. 1, (February 1995): 186–88.

DOCUMENTARIES AND TV PROGRAMS

A CBS News Inquiry: The Warren Report: June 25–28, 1967. 206 minutes. DVD. CBS, 2013.

As It Happened: JFK Assassination. 208 minutes. DVD. CBS, 2013.

CNN: The Sixties. The Decade That Changed the World: "The Assassination of President Kennedy." 85 minutes. DVD. Produced by Jonathan Buss and Stephen J. Morrison. Fremantle Media, 2015.

The Day Kennedy Died. 82 minutes. DVD. Produced by Lorraine McKechnie. Smithsonian Channel, 2013.

11.22.63. 450 minutes, DVD. Produced by John David Coles, et al. Warner Home Video, 2016.

Fatal Deception: Mrs. Lee Harvey Oswald. 91 minutes. DVD. Produced by Paul Pompian. Warner Archives Collection, 2013.

Frontline: Who Was Lee Harvey Oswald? 113 minutes. DVD. Produced by William Cran and Ben Loeterman. InVision Productions, 2013.

Hawaii Five-O. "Elua la ma Nowempa." Season 7, Episode 9. 44 minutes. DVD. Directed by Maja Vrvilo. CBS Television Distribution, 2016.

Image of An Assassination: A New Look at the Zapruder Film. 88 minutes. DVD. Produced by H.D. Motyl, et al. MPI Home Video, 1998.

JFK Assassination: The Definitive Guide. 90 minutes. DVD. Produced by Tony Bacon and Owen Palmquist. Lionsgate, 2013.

JFK: The Final Hours. 90 minutes. DVD. Produced by Robert Erickson. National Geographic Channel, 2013.

JFK: The Lost Bullet. 50 minutes. DVD. Produced by Robert Stone. Vivendi Entertainment, 2011.

JFK: One PM Central Standard Time. 90 minutes. DVD. Produced by Alastair Layzell. PBS, 2013.

JFK: Three Shots That Changed America. 188 minutes. DVD. Produced by Hugo Soskin, et al. New Video, 2010.

Kennedy. 350 minutes. DVD. Produced by Andrew Brown, et al. MPI Home Video, 2009.

The Kennedys. 353 minutes. DVD. Produced by John Cassar, et al. Lionsgate, 2011.

Killing Kennedy. 87 minutes. DVD. Produced by Larry Rapaport. 20th Century Fox Home Entertainment, 2014.

Lee Harvey Oswald: 48 Hours to Live. 96 minutes. DVD. Produced by Anthony Giacchino. History Channel, 2013.

The Lost JFK Tapes: The Assassination. 90 minutes. DVD. Produced by Tom Jennings. Vivendi Entertainment, 2009.

On Trial: Lee Harvey Oswald. 330 minutes. DVD. Produced by Mark Redhead. MPI Home Video, 2008.

Oswald's Ghost. 90 minutes. DVD. Produced by Robert Stone. PBS, 2008.

Pearl Harbor: 24 Hours After. 80 minutes. DVD. Produced by Anthony Giacchino. Lionsgate, 2012.

Quantum Leap. "Lee Harvey Oswald-October 5, 1957-November 22, 1963." Season 5, Episodes 1 & 2. 94 minutes. DVD. Directed by James Whitmore Jr. NBC Universal Television, 1992.

Ruby and Oswald. 100 minutes. DVD. Produced by Paul Freeman. Fremantle Media, 2007.

Seinfeld. "The Boyfriend." Season 3, Episodes 17 & 18. 47 minutes. DVD. Directed by Tom Cherones. Columbia Pictures Television, 1992.

The Simpsons. "Mayored to the Mob." Season 10, Episode 9. 23 minutes. DVD. Directed by Swinton O. Scott III. 20th Century, 1998.

South Park. "Weight Gain 4000." Season 1, Episode 2. 22 minutes. DVD. Directed by Trey Parker and Matt Stone. Paramount Global Distribution, 1997.

The Umbrella Academy. "Right Back Where We Started." Season 2, Episode 1. 47 minutes. DVD. Directed by Sylvain White. NBC Distribution and Netflix, 2020.

The X-Files. "Musings of a Cigarette Smoking Man." Season 4, Episode 7. 45 minutes. DVD. Directed by James Wong. 20th Century, 1996.

FILMS

Blow Out. 108 minutes. DVD. Directed by Brian De Palma. Criterion Collection, 2011.

Bubba Ho-Tep. 92 minutes. DVD. Directed by Don Cascarelli. MGM, 2004.

Executive Action. 91 minutes. DVD. Directed by David Miller. Warner Home Video, 2007.

Flashpoint. 94 minutes. DVD. Directed by William Tannen. HBO Archives, 2013.

In the Line of Fire. 129 minutes. DVD. Directed by Wolfgang Peterson. Sony Pictures Home Entertainment, 2001.

Interview with the Assassin. 88 minutes. DVD. Directed by Neil Burger. Showtime Entertainment, 2003.

The Irishman. 209 minutes. DVD. Directed by Martin Scorsese. Criterion Collection, 2020.

Jackie. 100 minutes. DVD. Directed by Pablo Larrain. Fox Searchlight Pictures, 2017.

JFK. 189 minutes. DVD. Directed by Oliver Stone. Warner Home Video, 1997.

John F. Kennedy: Years of Lightning, Day of Drums. 85 minutes. DVD. Directed by Bruce Herschensohn. Warner Home Video, 2013.

Love Field. 105 minutes. DVD. Directed by Jonathan Kaplan. MGM, 2001.

National Treasure. 131 minutes. DVD. Directed by Jon Turteltaub. Walt Disney Video, 2005.

The Parallax View. 102 minutes. DVD. Directed by Alan J. Pakula. Criterion Collection, 2021.

Parkland. 94 minutes. DVD. Directed by Peter Landesman. Exclusive Media, 2013.

The Rock. 136 minutes. DVD. Directed by Michael Bay. Hollywood Pictures Home Entertainment, 1997.

Ruby. 100 minutes. DVD. Directed by John MacKenzie. Sony Pictures Home Entertainment, 2003.

The Tall Target. 78 minutes. DVD. Directed by Anthony Mann, Warner Home Video, 2009.

Winter Kills. 97 minutes. DVD. Directed by William Richert. Anchor Bay, 2003.

X-Men: Days of Future Past. 132 minutes. DVD. Directed by Bryan Singer. 20th Century Fox Home Entertainment, 2014.

WEB ARTICLES

Bellamy, Jay. "A Stalwart of Stalwarts: Garfield's Assassin Sees Deed as a Special Duty." *Prologue Magazine*. Fall 2016, https://www.archives.gov/publications/prologue/2016/fall/quiteau.

Cartwright, Gary. "Who Was Jack Ruby?" *Texas Monthly.* November 1, 1975, https://www.texasmonthly.com/news-politics/who-was-jack-ruby.

Cohen, Andrew. "How to Watch the Kennedy Assassination Coverage as It Happened." *The Atlantic.* November 18, 2013, https://www.theatlantic.com/national/archive/2021/11/how-watch-the-kennedy-assassination-coverage-as-it-happened/281568.

Flynn, Tom. "Who Really Killed JFK? Experts Pick the Wildest Conspiracy Theories." *The Daily Beast.* November 20, 2013, https://www.thedailybeast.com/who-really-killed-jfk-experts-pick-the-wildest-conspiracy-theories.

Garza, Lisa Maria, et al. "Factbox: Quotes on 50th Anniversary of Kennedy's Assassination." *Reuters.* November 22, 2013, https://www.reuters.com/article/ususa-jfk-factbox-idUSBRE9AL14L20131122.

Herskovitz, Jon. "How the JFK Assassination Transformed Media Coverage." Reuters. November 21, 2013, https://www.reuters.com/article/us-usa-jfk-media-idUSBRE9AK11N20131122.

Langmann, Brady. "*The Irishman* Makes a Subtle Reference to the Mafia's Suspected Involvement in JFK's Assassination." *Esquire.* October 1, 2019, https://www.esquire.com/entertainment/movies/a29322953/the-irishman-jfk-assassination-mob-mafia-theory-frank-sheeran-true-story.

Shenon, Philip. "The Spy Chief Who Lied." *Politico.* October 6, 2015, https://www.politico.com/magazine/story/2015/10/jfk-assassination-john-mccone-warren-commission-cia-213197.

Spinelli, Dan. "Trump Revives Rumor Linking Cruz's Father to JFK Assassination." *Politico.* July 22, 2016, https://www.politico.com/story/2016-07/trump-ted-cruz-jfk-assassination-226020.

Tau, Byron. "Kerry Won't Talk About Kennedy Conspiracy." *Politico.* November 10, 2013, https://www.politico.com/blogs/politico-now/2013/11/kerry-wont-talk-about-kennedy-conspiracy-177167.

WEBSITES

IMDB (Internet Movie Database), https://www.imdb.com.